W9-CLL-571

Abusing Over-the-Counter Drugs
Illicit Uses for Everyday Drugs

ILLICIT AND MISUSED DRUGS

ILLICIT AND MISUSED DRUGS

Abusing Over-the-Counter Drugs

Illicit Uses for Everyday Drugs

by Kim Etingoff

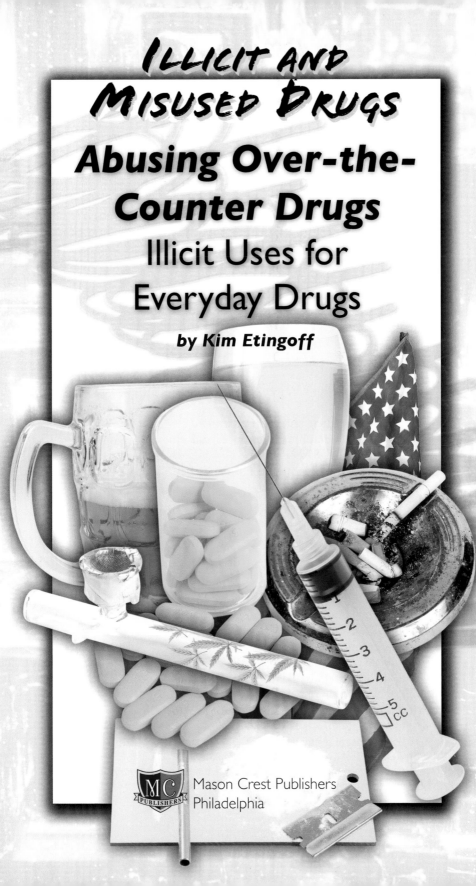

Mason Crest Publishers
Philadelphia

Mason Crest Publishers Inc.
370 Reed Road
Broomall, Pennsylvania 19008
(866) MCP-BOOK (toll free)
www.masoncrest.com

First printing
1 2 3 4 5 6 7 8 9 10
Library of Congress Cataloging-in-Publication Data
ISBN-13: 978-1-4222-0149-7 (series)

Etingoff, Kim.
    Abusing over-the-counter drugs : illicit uses for everyday drugs /
by Kim Etingoff.
      p. cm. — (Illicit and misused drugs)
    Includes bibliographical references and index.
    ISBN-13: 978-1-4222-0150-3
    1. Drug abuse—Juvenile literature. 2. Drugs, Nonprescription—
Juvenile literature.   I. Title.
    HV5809.5.E85 2008
    613.8—dc22
                                                            2006030112

Interior design by Benjamin Stewart.
Cover design by MK Bassett-Harvey.
Produced by Harding House Publishing Service Inc.
Vestal, New York.
www.hardinghousepages.com

Cover image design by Peter Spires Culotta.
Cover photography: Dreamstime
Printed in the Hashemite Kingdom of Jordan.

CONTENTS

INTRODUCTION

Addicting drugs are among the greatest challenges to health, well-being, and the sense of independence and freedom for which we all strive—and yet these drugs are present in the everyday lives of most people. Almost every home has alcohol or tobacco waiting to be used, and has medicine cabinets stocked with possibly outdated but still potentially deadly drugs. Almost everyone has a friend or loved one with an addiction-related problem. Almost everyone seems to have a solution neatly summarized by word or phrase: medicalization, legalization, criminalization, war-on-drugs.

For better and for worse, drug information seems to be everywhere, but what information sources can you trust? How do you separate misinformation (whether deliberate or born of ignorance and prejudice) from the facts? Are prescription drugs safer than "street" drugs? Is occasional drug use really harmful? Is cigarette smoking more addictive than heroin? Is marijuana safer than alcohol? Are the harms caused by drug use limited to the users? Can some people become addicted following just a few exposures? Is treatment or counseling just for those with serious addiction problems?

These are just a few of the many questions addressed in this series. It is an empowering series because it provides the information and perspectives that can help people come to their own opinions and find answers to the challenges posed by drugs in their own lives. The series also provides further resources for information and assistance, recognizing that no single source has all the answers. It should be of interest and relevance to areas of study spanning biology, chemistry, history, health, social studies and more. Its efforts to provide a real-world context for the information that is clearly presented but not overly simplified should be appreciated by students, teachers, and parents.

The series is especially commendable in that it does not pretend to pose easy answers or imply that all decisions can be made on the basis of simple facts: some challenges have no immediate or simple solutions, and some solutions will need to rely as much upon basic values as basic facts. Despite this, the series should help to at least provide a foundation of knowledge. In the end, it may help as much by pointing out where the solutions are not simple, obvious, or known to work. In fact, at many points, the reader is challenged to think for him- or herself by being asked what his or her opinion is.

A core concept of the series is to recognize that we will never have all the facts, and many of the decisions will never be easy. Hopefully, however, armed with information, perspective, and resources, readers will be better prepared for taking on the challenges posed by addictive drugs in everyday life.

— *Jack E. Henningfield, Ph.D.*

1 What Are Over-the-Counter Drugs?

When the word "drug" comes to mind, people either conjure up images of illegal substances like cocaine and heroin—or they think of medical drugs. But while people may distinguish between these two categories of drugs, a growing trend links the two: over-the-counter (OTC) drug abuse.

OTC drugs are substances that alter the body for medical purposes but that don't need a doctor's prescription to be purchased. This category of drugs includes some medicines that treat headaches, colds, coughing, and allergies. Common medicines such as Advil®, Tylenol®, and Robitussin® are all classified as over-the-counter drugs.

While these medicines may seem innocent enough, more and more people are intentionally misusing them.

OTC drug abuse is on the rise. Between 2000 and 2003, the American Association of Poison Control Centers cited a doubling in OTC drug-related calls to U.S. poison control centers. Emergency room visits having to do with OTC drug abuse have also increased dramatically. Nor is this abuse just a problem contained in North America. Countries around the world have also seen a rise in abuse. In Switzerland, the Swiss Toxicological Information Center saw a rise in calls relating to OTC products, which are easily bought in stores and on the street.

Instead of seeking the drugs' medicinal benefits, users want to experience the highs that accompany taking large amounts of some OTC drugs. Unfortunately, these habits are **detrimental** to users' health. In fact, they can be just as serious as illegal drug abuse.

Deadly Cough Syrup

One of the most commonly abused OTC drugs is dextromethorphan, referred to as DXM. This drug is found in many cold medicines that are in either liquid or capsule form, especially those treating coughing. Currently, over 120 medicines contain DXM. These include Robitussin, Vicks NyQuil®, and Coricidin HBP®. Because Robitussin is one of the most commonly abused cough medicines, DXM abuse is sometimes referred to as robo-tripping. The drug itself has several street names, including Robo, Orange Crush, Skittles, and Dex. Another name, Triple-C, refers specifically to Coricidin HBP Cough and Cold, considered to be one of the most dangerous OTC drugs to abuse. It contains thirty milligrams of DXM per tablet, while other medicines such as Robitussin DM® contain two milligrams per milliliter of syrup.

Abuse occurs when a user purposefully takes more than the recommended amount of medicine. Generally,

Brand Name vs. Generic Name

Talking about medications can be confusing because every drug has at least two names: its "generic name" and the "brand name" that the pharmaceutical company uses to market the drug. Generic names are based on the drug's chemical structure, while drug companies use brand names to inspire public recognition and loyalty for their products.

Many cough medicines contain dextromethorphan (DXM), a commonly abused OTC drug.

abusers simply drink cough syrup or take liquid pills containing cough medicine. Less commonly, people may ingest it in powdered form, which can be bought on the Internet. Accepted doses for those who are using medicines containing DXM with the intention of treating a medical condition are fifteen to thirty milligrams per use. Abusers consume many times that amount to get high off DXM. For example, even light users may use 100 to 200 milligrams, while heavy users may use 600 to 1500 milligrams at one time. The effects of DXM use generally last from four to six hours, depending on how much was taken, with larger doses producing more *profound* effects for longer periods of time.

Abusers of products containing DXM want to experience certain effects that taking large doses has on the body. DXM, an opium derivative, is a type of drug called a dissociative, meaning that it blocks signals from the

A Short List of OTC Medicines with DXM

Alka-Seltzer Plus Cold & Cough Medicine®
Contac®
Coricidin HBP Cough and Cold
Dayquil LiquiCaps®
Delsym®
Dimetapp DM®
Drixoral®
Pertussin®
Robitussin
Sudafed®
Triaminic®
Tylenol Cold
Vicks 44 Cough Relief
Vicks NyQuil LiquiCaps

DXM is a derivative of opium, a drug that comes from a kind of poppy.

DXM is an antitussive, designed to combat coughing and other symptoms of a cold. When taken correctly, it is safe even for children.

One way that some users choose to take DXM is called robo shaking. This practice involves drinking large amounts of cough syrup and then forcibly throwing up. The DXM is absorbed into the body through the stomach, but the vomiting expels other, unwanted ingredients in the cough syrup. Some users even go so far as to use chemical processes to extract pure DXM from liquid cough medicines as a method to avoid those undesirable ingredients.

consciousness to parts of the brain that control physical processes like vision and movement. Because of this, taking DXM creates feelings of being disconnected from reality and from one's self. While under the influence of DXM, people feel *euphoria*, often laugh a lot, live in a dream-like state, and feel forgiving and affectionate toward other people.

A Different Drug at Different Amounts

Dextromethorphan, as found in cough and cold medicines, is generally a safe and beneficial drug; it is only dangerous if used beyond the suggested dosage listed on the product package. In fact, cough medicines are generally extremely safe with very few side effects. Because of their safety record, they are sold directly to consumers who have determined that they need the medicine. It is an accepted practice for people with colds, allergies, and headaches to treat themselves with OTC drugs; there is no need for a doctor to write a prescription.

DXM is an antitussive, a medicine that combats coughing. In small amounts, it treats coughing, itchy throats, runny noses, and congestion from colds, allergies, and the flu. It begins to work after approximately fifteen to thirty minutes, and acts to alleviate coughing for three to six hours.

Over-the-counter drugs do not require a doctor's prescription to buy; they are the medications available in any drugstore.

Chapter 1—What Are Over-the-Counter Drugs?

OTC medicines containing dextromethorphan are easily identified. Often, the medicine contains the word "tuss" in its name, referring to the classification of its type of substance: an antitussive drug, or one that reduces coughing. At other times, the labeling may use the terms "DX" or "maximum strength." Additionally, all medicines containing DXM will list it under the active ingredients found in the product.

However, DXM becomes dangerous when taken in higher-than-accepted doses. Users describe four stages, or plateaus, of DXM abuse. The first plateau, corresponding to lower doses of DXM, includes mild euphoria and impairment. Users experiencing the intermediate plateaus lose motor skills and control of their senses, have stronger euphoric feelings, and may start to **hallucinate**. The first and intermediate plateaus are sometimes compared to the effects of drinking alcohol to the point of drunkenness. The highest plateau, caused by the ingestion of extremely large amounts of DXM, can lead to out-of-body experiences and extreme hallucinations. Users compare this plateau to being high on **ketamine** or **PCP**.

DXM's History

Since it is a **synthetic** substance, dextromethorphan has a relatively short history. After its initial creation, the U.S. Food and Drug Administration (FDA) approved DXM in 1958, introducing the drug, in a form called Romilar, to consumers. After its introduction, DXM slowly became the most popular cough medicine, replacing **codeine**, which was then being used to treat coughs. This particular form of cough suppressant was discontinued in 1975, after studies showed that its abuse was increasing. Later, other products with DXM were created, but this time, manufacturers made sure that their medicines tasted bad to discourage abuse. However, abuse is now on the rise again, possibly due in part to the addition of flavoring to the medicines, making them more appealing. As of 2007, products containing DXM are still legal to buy and possess without a prescription and they are not part of the drug scheduling system in place in the United States, set up in 1970.

The fact that they are still available doesn't mean they are as easy to obtain as they once were. In 2005, the Federal Combat Methamphetamine Act was approved. As of September 30, 2006, retailers were required to follow strict employee training, product placement, identification, and logbook procedures connected with the purchase of any OTC medication that can be used in the production of methamphetamine, including DXM. Sales

The History of Aspirin

Hippocrates, the father of modern medicine, who lived sometime between 460 and 377 BCE, left historical records of a powder made from the bark and leaves of the willow tree. He used this powder to relieve headaches and other pains. Native Americans also recognized the medical properties of the willow tree; they chewed the willow's leaves and inner bark or boiled a tea made from them to relieve fever or other minor pain like toothaches, headaches, or arthritis. By 1829, scientists discovered that it was the compound called salicin in willow plants that provided the pain relief. A German company called Bayer patented aspirin on March 6, 1889. The folks at Bayer came up with the name aspirin, using the "a" in acetyl chloride (the chemical compound contained in salicin), the "spir" in spiraea ulmaria (the genus of plant containing this compound) and "in," which was a then familiar name ending for medicines. Aspirin was first sold as a powder, but in 1915, the first aspirin tablets were made.

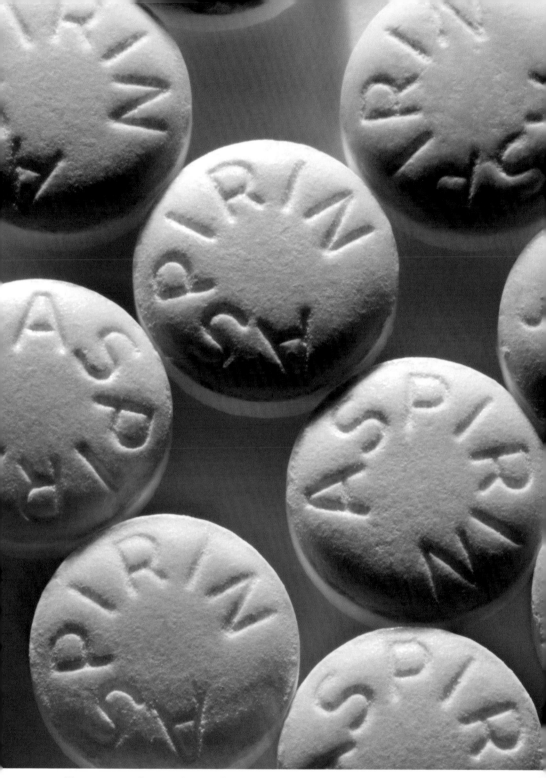

The aspirin we know today was first manufactured in 1915—but for more than two thousand years, the chemical contained in this OTC medicine has been known to be effective for relieving headaches and other pain.

The Internet makes many drugs more easily accessible—and even offers
instructions on how to abuse them.

20 Chapter 1—What Are Over-the-Counter Drugs?

restrictions were put in place on April 8, 2006. Most of these medications are now placed behind the counter, and individuals are limited as to how much they can buy at one time or within thirty days.

As well intentioned as these new regulations are, they are not without their own problems. According to journalist Sarah Fenske of the Phoenix *New Times*, Arizona's government was convinced that if they cut the supply of the ingredients used to make crystal meth—namely, OTC cold medicines—the demand would drop as well.

But when a law went into effect that regulated all cold medicines containing pseudoephedrine—one of the key ingredients meth cooks use—the results took them by surprise. Under the new law, everything from Sudafed to Tylenol Cold has to be kept behind the counter, and customers must sign a logbook that is faxed monthly to the police.

As the cops read through the logs, they kept noticing the same name over and over at the same address in a small town outside Phoenix. So the police went out to investigate. They were ready to bust a ring of meth cookers.

Instead, they found a large family with the flu.

In today's world, the Internet has acted as a new tool to spread DXM abuse. The freedom of the Internet allows people to set up sites promoting its use, telling users how much to take and how to get high. Some even have charts and calculators to help people take the amount of DXM necessary to get high, based on age and weight. Sites called pill mills also make it easier for users to get their drug of choice. These "pharmacies" do not require buyers to have prescriptions or even to travel to a store to buy medicine. This allows people to easily buy a large supply of medicine without alerting suspicion.

This information has led to a shift in preferred methods of consuming DXM. Before the advent of easy-to-get instructions on how to use DXM more efficiently and effectively, users would drink entire bottles of cough syrup, which was unpleasant and could produce vomiting. Today, with better information and the possibility of buying powdered DXM online, more users are choosing to use this form of the drug and snort it.

Other OTC Drugs Being Abused

DXM is not the only OTC drug now on the menu for individuals looking for a high. Painkillers, or *analgesics*, are another common category of OTC drugs that are subject to abuse. Normally, these medications combat muscle aches, headaches, menstrual cramps, and the pain of everyday bumps and bruises. Acetaminophen, better known as Tylenol®; acetylsalicylic acid (ASA), or aspirin; and ibuprofen, found in Advil®, are some of the more commonly abused analgesics. If taken in large amounts, these medicines all create feelings of euphoria and hallucinations similar to products containing DXM.

Antihistamines are yet another category of abused OTC drugs. Antihistamines are used to treat allergies and *acute* allergic reactions. Antihistamines are also sometimes found in sleep aids and motion sickness pills. Like DXM and analgesics, they also produce a type of high if taken in excess. Abuse of these medicines, such as Tylenol PM and Excedrin PM, is not uncommon. People who wish to experience the hallucinogenic effects of these drugs usually have to take large amounts, sometimes whole packs of medicine at a time. Motion sickness pills like Dramamine® are also being abused because of the

Drinking an entire bottle of cough medicine is not pleasant and can cause nausea or vomiting.

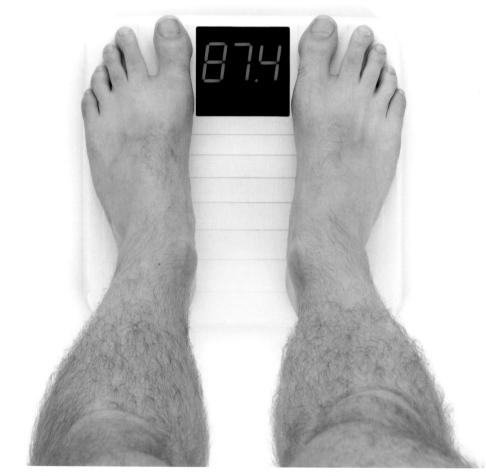

Our modern culture is preoccupied with dieting; as a result, OTC diet pills are popular with people seeking a quick and easy answer to their weight issues. Such pills are not necessarily safe.

hallucinogenic effects they can have when taken in large amounts.

Extreme Dieting

Getting high is not the only criteria for drug abuse. Many people who are overly concerned with losing weight misuse drugs to achieve their goals. Instead of dieting and exercise, diet pills have become a popular way of losing weight. While diet pills may not be as physically addicting as some other drugs such as cocaine or heroin, people can still become psychologically dependent on them. This type of addiction is similar to caffeine dependence, but more extreme and with more serious consequences.

Abuse of diet pills is a relatively new phenomenon. At some times in history, plumpness was considered a sign of health and beauty, even of prosperity. But during the last few decades, that image has shifted, until today being thin—and the thinner the better—is equated with being beautiful. There has been a corresponding increase in the desire to lose weight, and an increasing number of ways to do so. The first diet pill was introduced to the public in 1893, and today there are hundreds of OTC diet pills available, many with dangerous side effects. Many people are willing to believe that pills will miraculously let them lose weight and never think to research what may be in those pills, a potentially deadly mistake.

Many diet pills, although seemingly harmless because they may be advertised as containing natural ingredients, can be surprisingly dangerous when taken in large doses. Diet pills often contain substances that are similar to amphetamines (drugs sometimes known as uppers, which are often abused). Both amphetamines and the substances

Ephedrine is a common ingredient in many medications used to treat asthma.

found in diet pills are appetite suppressants. These drugs send a chemical to the brain telling the individual she is full, even though her body may still be hungry.

Anorectic drugs, appetite suppressants, are also found in diet pills such as fenfluramine (or fen-phen), phentermine, diethylproprion, and mazindol. Perhaps the most hazardous ingredient commonly found in diet pills until a few years ago was ephedrine. Ephedrine is more commonly known as one of the *precursor* chemicals needed to manufacture methamphetamine.

Ephedrine: No Longer OTC

Until recently, ephedrine was the most popular OTC weight-loss remedy. The FDA has in fact approved one form of ephedrine—ephedrine hydrochloride—but this is the only type of ephedrine that can be legally considered a drug, and this form is not found in weight-loss products. The most common form used in non-FDA–approved products is an *extract* from a plant found in the United States. A similar plant exists in China as well.

A *stimulant* that affects the nervous system, ephedrine has been used for decades as a component of nasal decongestants and asthma treatments. Ephedrine is also well known in athletic circles for its performance-enhancing properties. It causes high blood pressure and elevated heart rate, and is believed to increase the *metabolism* of those taking it for extended periods of time. This gives athletes more energy and allows calories to be burned more quickly.

Ephedrine has been linked to several deaths. As a result, it has been banned until more research can be done. Ephedrine may cause severe bleeding in the brain, as well as sudden heart attacks and strokes. It is a good example

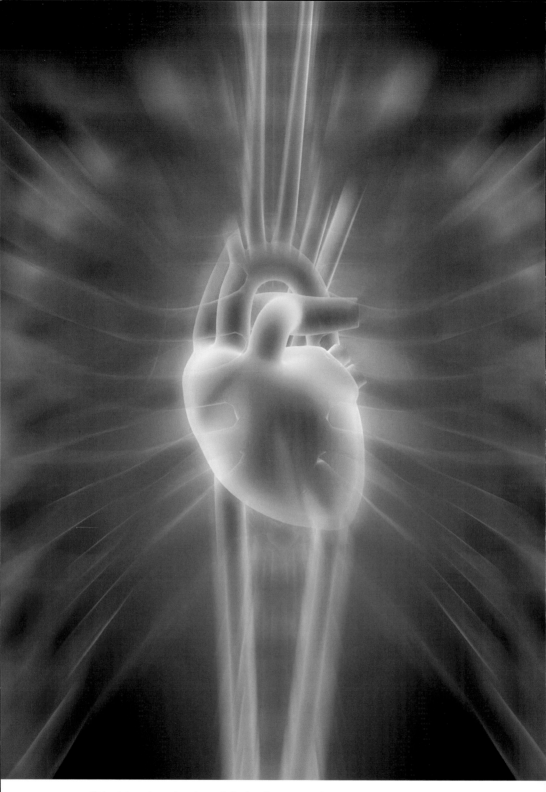

Ephedrine abuse has been linked to heart attacks.

of an over-the-counter drug that eventually proved to be far more dangerous than anyone had ever suspected.

Weight Loss Beyond Diet Pills: Laxatives and Diuretics

Diet pills are not the only OTC drugs that are abused in the battle to achieve weight loss. Laxatives are another substance that people use to lose weight. Normally, people use laxatives to relieve constipation, since they act to irritate intestinal linings and stimulate nerves. Abusers believe that they help them lose weight by rushing food through their bodies. However, laxatives do not actually aid in weight loss, since the nutrients and calories in food, the real culprits in weight gain, have already been taken in by the body before the medicine begins to work. Ironically, because laxatives do not actually work, users feel the need to continue to take them in increasing amounts in the hope that they do. This eventually leads to dependence.

Diuretics, or water pills, are abused in a similar way to laxatives. They act by forcing the body to lose fluids, creating the feeling that the user is really losing weight. When the body naturally begins to regain the lost water, people take more medicine. Again, because diuretics do not actually work as the abuser intended, he or she continues to take them.

Other people turn to a different method of forced weight loss. Individuals with bulimia, an eating disorder in which vomiting is induced after eating in order to prevent food from being absorbed by the body, sometimes use drugs as part of their illness. In particular, a medicinal syrup called ipecac causes abusers to vomit. Ipecac, an

Ginseng root is an example of a natural remedy that may in fact be an effective health aid.

extract found in the ipecacuanha shrub that grows in Brazil, stimulates the central nervous system, which sends messages to the stomach, forcing vomiting. It is only meant to be used in cases of serious poisoning, not on a daily basis by people who wish to lose weight.

Weight Loss the "Natural" Way

Many over-the-counter treatments are herbal supplements popularized by the recent trend toward all things "natural." In a grocery or department store, a shopper can buy a vast array of different herbal supplements, all reported to have some healing property or nutritional value. Ginseng, echinacea, ginger root, flaxseed oil, lavender oil, and shark cartilage are all examples of the things one can find, each with a different function that supposedly makes life better.

Herbal remedies are not necessarily bad. Research indicates that many are effective health aids. The problem with over-the-counter remedies, however, is that they are not thoroughly tested. The manufacturers rely on word-of-mouth—and infomercials on television—to sell their products, and they don't wish to pay the large amounts of money to conduct the research and testing required to pass the rigorous FDA-testing procedures. Although this keeps prices down for consumers, it also allows manufactures to get rich quick, without complying with FDA regulations. Lacking FDA approval allows the manufacturers to market their products as nondrugs, which largely frees them of the burden of having to provide information to the public about the real effectiveness—or dangers—of the product.

Ordinary dandelion—the weed that grows so abundantly on many lawns—is also used as a natural weight-loss supplement. Unfortunately, it can cause dehydration and possibly even cancer.

Aloe

Perhaps one of the most surprising weight-loss supplements recently produced is aloe. Long used to treat burns and wounds, it was discovered that ingesting aloe causes a strong and urgent need to defecate. Because of that effect, aloe is often marketed as an internal cleanser. Supplements that cause reactions like this are not likely to be safe to take internally, as diarrhea is a warning sign of some potentially dangerous conditions. No proof has been offered that aloe is useful in losing and keeping off weight.

Dandelion

Dandelion—yes, those fuzzy yellow flowers that dot the lawn—has also recently entered the market as a weight-loss supplement. A natural diuretic, dandelion causes frequent urination and can reduce the water weight a person carries. Many people are allergic to this supplement, and it can cause severe *dehydration* in long-term users. Some research has shown that dandelion may be carcinogenic, causing cancers in laboratory rats.

Guarana

In Brazil, native people have long known that the seeds of a certain plant have a stimulating effect when eaten or ground up and mixed with water or tea. Today, guarana is common in herbal remedy sections, as it speeds up metabolism and promotes frequent urination. One of the components of guarana extract is caffeine, which is known to cause high blood pressure. Guarana often interacts with medicines and can cause deadly complications in certain cases. The extract has some relatively powerful anti-clotting properties and can cause unstoppable bleeding in long-term users.

Although aloe is known to promote skin healing, it is probably not safe to take it internally to promote weight loss.

Guar Gum

The Indian cluster bean is the source of yet another powerful herbal extract. Guar gum is a type of dietary fiber, often used as a thickening substance in cooking or in medications. The action of guar gum is like a sponge; it absorbs water rapidly and swells up to twenty times its original size in the process. Some people who have used this substance to curb their appetites have had very dangerous intestinal blockages, requiring surgery to remove. Guar gum also causes rapid blood sugar changes, so diabetics must take extreme care in taking it.

If so many OTC drugs have the potential to be dangerous, why are they still so easy to purchase? The answer to that lies in the history of drug development in North America.

2 The History of Over-the-Counter Drugs

When did you last reach into your family's medicine cabinet? Did you have a headache and need some aspirin? Or did sneezing and sniffling send you in search of an antihistamine? Whatever your reason for taking medication, you probably felt confident that what you were about to take was safe, that it was, indeed, what the package said it was, and that it would do what the manufacturer said it would do.

But how would you feel if you took an aspirin, only to discover that it wasn't aspirin at all but compacted chalk dust? What if you swallowed an allergy pill—and learned that it not only didn't help but also made your allergies worse? Imagine what it would be like to take a liquid antibiotic only to discover that it was antifreeze for your car. These scenarios seem impossible today—but less than a hundred years ago, they were all too possible.

Despite its innocent and wholesome image, alcohol was a key ingredient in Lydia Pinkham's Vegetable Compound.

Nineteenth-Century Medicines

Prior to the Food, Drug and Cosmetic Act of 1938, the United States had few laws governing medicines, drug development, and drug distribution. In the late 1800s, *patent medicines* reigned supreme. Medicine show "professors" traveled around North America, hawking their miraculous, exotic "cures" from soapboxes or platforms in carnival tents. These medicine men brought North America everything from Foley's Honey and Tar (for coughs and colds) to Hot Springs Liver Buttons (which promised to keep "your liver all right and your bowels regular"). The audience listened and purchased these cures because the products promised "health in a bottle" during a time of limited access to good medical care.

"Feeling weak?" the salesmen would cry. "Have digestive problems? Suffer from blood disorders or nervous conditions? No need for a doctor! Just try Dr. Williams' Pink Pills for Pale People. This little pill will cure what ails you, and may even save your life! Only fifty cents a box, six boxes for $2.50."

Some Early Patent Medicines and Their Claims

• Lydia Pinkham's Vegetable Compound, a brew of herbs and alcohol, claimed to treat menstrual cramps and cure other women's ills.

• Hamlin's Wizard Oil Company's cure-all, The Great Medical Wonder, promised to cure headaches within five minutes, earaches in ten, and nerve disorders in fifteen. Its advertisements read, "There is no Sore it will Not Heal, No Pain it will not subdue."

• Dr. William's Pink Pills for Pale People was advertised to be a "safe and effective tonic for the blood and nerves." Its label claimed that the pills treated anemic conditions, nervous disorders, and conditions caused by thin blood.

A popular patent medicine of the 1890s, Dr. Williams' pink-pill cure was only one of many patent medicines sold during the late nineteenth century. According to Dr. Tina Brewster Wray, the Curator of Collections at the White River Valley Museum in Auburn, Washington, medicine merchants marketed over 100,000 brands of patent medicines between 1860 and 1900. But these so-called cures were nothing new.

Patent medicines arrived in the North America in the late 1700s as medicines that had been produced under grants from the English king. Under these grants, which were called "patents," the king gave his official permission for the manufacturer to develop the medicine, and he promised to provide royal financial backing. Hence the name, "patent medicine." Though usually referred to as patent medicines, the actual medicines (their recipe and ingredient list) weren't patented in North America as we think of patents today; only the medicine's name and packaging were registered with the government as a trademark to protect the remedy's owner and manufacturer. The ingredient list and recipe remained secret. And that was a problem.

Most patent medicine ingredients weren't medicines at all. Though they claimed to cure everything from diaper rash to diabetes, they were often nothing more than alcohol, flavorings, herbs, or narcotics mixed together and put in a colorful bottle or box with an impressive-looking label.

Some labels and advertisements made ridiculous claims, like those made by Warner's Safe Liver and Kidney Cure, which claimed that Warner's medicine could treat all diseases of the lower half of the body. Another patent medicine, Wintersmith's Chill Tonic, claimed to

In the 1800s, medicines' advertisements did not have to prove their claims.

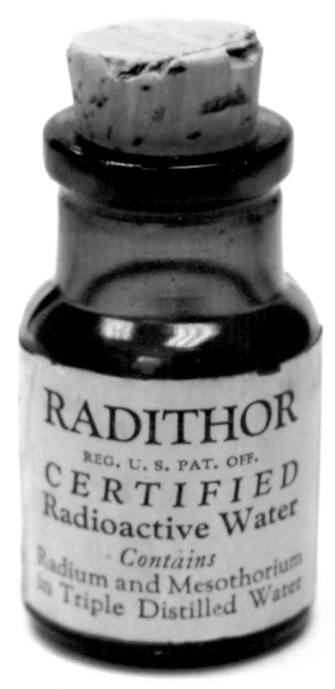

Radithor contained a radioactive ingredient that ate away teeth and bones—and eventually, could prove to be fatal.

cure malaria—a remarkable claim for the early 1890s, considering that the World Health Organization still attributes more than one million deaths annually to malaria today.

Most patent medicines claimed to work miracles, but ultimately did nothing to heal people, and in some cases caused actual harm, as was the case with Pittsburgh millionaire and industrialist Eben Byers. In 1928, Mr. Byers injured himself at a post-game party following the annual Yale-Harvard football game. On the advice of his physician, Byers drank three half-ounce bottles per day of a patent medicine called Radithor to ease his pain and overcome his injury. He continued this treatment for two years, but stopped abruptly when his teeth started falling out. Though the manufacturer claimed that Radithor was "harmless in every respect," the concoction contained radium, a radioactive element, that not only caused Byers' loss of teeth but also ate away the bones of his jaw and skull. It caused his death in 1931.

According to the U.S. National Library of Medicine, one of the worst results of the ill effects of patent medicine use in the late nineteenth and early twentieth centuries was the number of healthy babies who became addicted to morphine, heroine, opium, or alcohol. How did babies develop these addictions? Well, imagine being a mother or father with an infant who won't stop crying. The baby shrieks night and day. You never get to sleep. You can't rest. You're exhausted and your child is miserable. As a parent, if you could find a cure for your baby's misery, would you buy it? Of course you would, just as thousands did at the turn of the twentieth century.

The problem was not with the parents but with the cure. Most "soothers" or "soothing syrups," as the patent medicines sold to calm crying children were called,

Medicine's Hall of Shame

- *Radithor.* This radioactive liquid sold as a patent medicine in the late 1920s ultimately led to the user's slow and painful death from radiation poisoning.
- *Lash Lure.* A cosmetic product of the 1930s, this eyelash dye blinded many women. One Lash Lure user died, all for want of lovely eyelashes.
- *Elixir Sulfanilamide.* Touted as a more palatable version of the sulfanilamide pill, this tasty liquid antibiotic released in 1937 resulted in more than a hundred deaths. Why? The liquid in which the medicine was dissolved was basically antifreeze.
- *Thalidomide.* All its tired users wanted was sleep. All its pregnant users wanted was relief from morning sickness. Though this medicine gave patients a good night's rest and settled their stomachs, it caused ten thousand children to be born horribly disfigured. Many thalidomide babies had no arms, legs, hands, and feet; they had only "flippers" attached to their shoulders and hips.

contained morphine, heroin, opium, or other addictive narcotics. These drug-laced syrups made children sleep, but the children also ended up addicted to the drug the syrups contained. Because no laws required manufacturers to list ingredients on a medicine's label, parents didn't know what was in the medicines they bought.

On October 7, 1905, a newspaper reporter, Samuel Hopkins Adams, published the first of a ten-week investigative report on the patent medicine industry for *Collier's Weekly*. Called "The Great American Fraud," his series of articles exposed the deceit and trickery of the patent medicine industry—how they were marketing and selling cures that weren't really cures at all. His articles also revealed the dangerous side effects of patent medicines and their inaccurate labeling. By using startling images of skulls and death superimposed over medicine bottles in his articles, Adams caught the public's attention; the public demanded action; and a new law was born.

On June 30, 1906, with the support of President Theodore Roosevelt, Congress passed the Pure Food and Drug Act of 1906. Because of this law, product labels now had to accurately list ingredients and ingredient strength. Medicine labels also had to declare the presence of narcotics, opiates, or other addictive drugs. For the first time in American history, consumers would know what they were getting in the medicines they purchased.

The Birth of the FDA

In the 1930s, a pharmaceutical company named S. E. Massengill produced a medication that proved helpful in

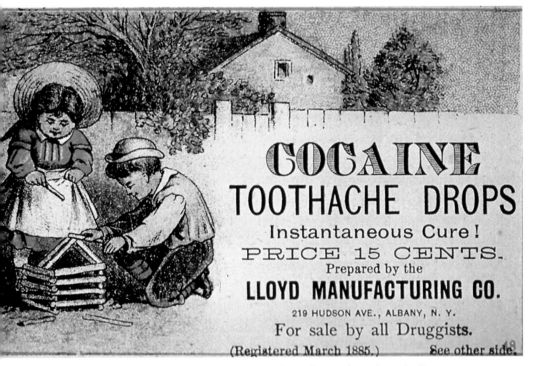

These innocent-looking toothache drops make no bones about their chief ingredient: cocaine!

fighting bacterial infections. The medication was called "sulfanilamide." Sulfanilamide, in pill form, tasted terrible and was difficult to swallow, so the manufacturer decided to produce the same medication in liquid form. In 1937, Massengill developed a liquid sulfanilamide solution, added some pink food coloring and cherry flavoring, and began selling the product to the public. Because of its bright color and appealing taste, the new medicine, now called Elixir Sulfanilamide, was especially useful for children. Parents bought the tasty solution for sons and daughters who had earaches, chest colds, sore throats, high fevers—anything caused by a bacterial infection. The pill form worked well; surely the liquid form of the same medication would work well, too.

Unfortunately, children treated with the new liquid didn't get well. They died. In all, 107 people died (mostly children) from taking Elixir Sulfanilamide. Why? The chemists who developed the elixir knew that sulfanilamide could not be dissolved in water so they used a different, untested liquid in which to dissolve the helpful drug. That liquid, which became the base for the new liquid medication, was called diethylene glycol. It was much like what we use in automobile antifreeze today. The liquid used to carry a beneficial drug to bacterial infections poisoned those who took it.

What happened when so many died? The chemist who developed Elixir Sulfanilamide was so distraught over the tragic deaths his medicine caused that he committed suicide. Massengill, the company who made and marketed the pink liquid, was fined $26,100 (the maximum fine legally allowed at that time), but not otherwise held liable. More important, an outraged public cried out for action, which resulted in the passage of a new law,

Elixir Sulfanilamide caused the death of 107 people. It contained an ingredient similar to antifreeze.

called the Food, Drug and Cosmetic Act of 1938. This new legislation required drug companies to prove that a new drug was safe before they could sell the drug to the public. For the first time in history, medicines would have to be tested and proved safe before release. Who would examine the proof? A government agency called the United States Food and Drug Administration, what today we refer to as the FDA.

The FDA Today: How Safe Is Safe?

Today's FDA is the primary consumer protection agency in the United States. Operating under the authority

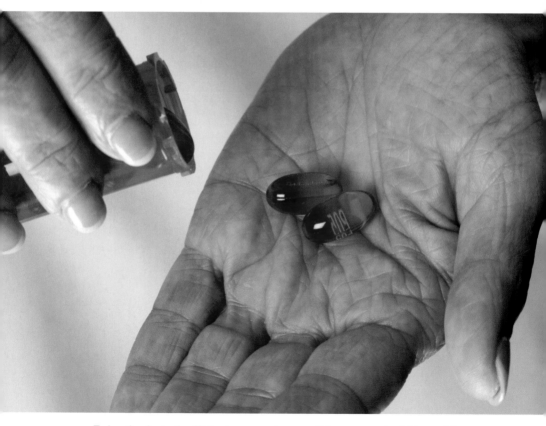

Today, thanks to the FDA, when we take a medicine, we can be fairly confident that it is safe and effective when used for its approved use.

Drug Approval in Canada

While the United States has the FDA for the approval and regulation of drugs and medical devices, Canada has a similar organization called the Therapeutic Product Directorate (TPD). The TPD is a division of Health Canada, the Canadian government's department of health. The TPD regulates drugs, medical devices, disinfectants, and sanitizers with disinfectant claims. Some of the things that the TPD monitors are quality, effectiveness, and safety. Just as the FDA must approve new drugs in the United States, the TPD must approve new drugs in Canada before those drugs can enter the market.

given it by the government, and guided by laws established throughout the twentieth century, the FDA has established a rigorous drug approval process that verifies the safety, effectiveness, and accuracy of labeling for any drug marketed in the United States.

When the FDA approves a drug, it is saying that the drug is safe and effective for public use when used as instructed. But "safe does not mean harmless," stated Janet Woodcock, M.D., director of the FDA's Center for Drug Evaluation and Research (CDER) in an interview with *FDA Consumer* magazine. "Every drug comes with risks, and our tolerance for risk is higher for drugs that treat serious and life-threatening illnesses. There is no question that cancer drugs can be highly toxic. But they also save lives."

The word safe, when applied to FDA-approved drugs, means only that the drug's effectiveness for its intended use (how well it works on the targeted disease or disorder) outweighs its risks (possible side effects). Generally speaking, if clinical studies show that a drug works and its side effects are tolerable, the drug will most likely be approved. If the drug works but kills or seriously harms the patients taking it, the drug will most likely not be

According to the Dietary Supplement Health and Education Act of 1994, a dietary ingredient may include:

- a vitamin
- a mineral
- an herb or other botanical
- an amino acid
- a dietary substance for use to supplement the diet by increasing the total dietary intake
- a concentrate, metabolite, constituent, or extract

approved. The risk of taking the drug has to be worth the benefit the drug provides. And that's the case for most drugs on the market.

Before approving a drug, the FDA tries to find out about the drug's potential risks. Many side effects show up in the manufacturer's preapproval studies and are noted in the application made to the FDA. But what if a particular reaction happens in only one out of twenty-five thousand people? Or in one out of fifty thousand? Most *clinical trials* test drugs on only a few hundred to several thousand people. A serious reaction that occurs once in twenty-five thousand times or once in fifty thousand may be missed in these studies. That side effect might remain unknown until tens or hundreds of thousands of people—a number far greater than the average number of people involved in clinical trials—have used the drug.

Though they endeavor to do so, the FDA and drug manufacturers can't anticipate every possible side effect of a drug in every person. Even the safest drugs, when used appropriately, can cause adverse reactions.

An adverse reaction is an unintended, unwanted side effect. It can be unpleasant or harmful, or it may just be unexpected. You can have adverse reactions to many different things: for instance, drugs, medical devices, vaccines, cosmetics, herbs, vitamins, and food. These reactions can range from the mildly irritating to life threatening. Common mild adverse reactions to drugs include stomach upset, drowsiness, dizziness, restlessness, difficulty sleeping, headache, rash, abdominal pain, and diarrhea.

New drugs and old drugs alike can cause adverse reactions. Over-the-counter antihistamines (like Benedryl),

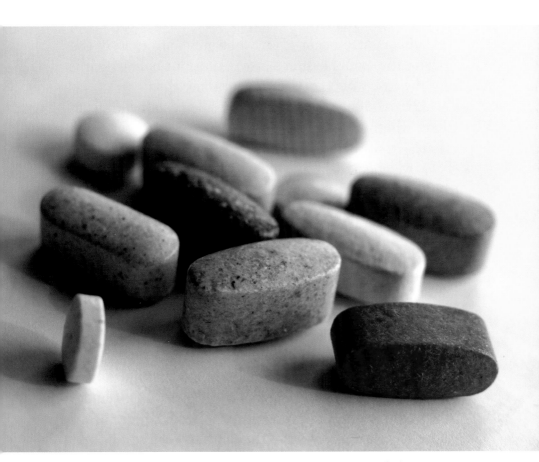

Vitamins are examples of dietary supplements that are not classified as medicines.

for example, do a great job combating allergies but can cause extreme drowsiness (not a big deal unless you are driving a car or operating dangerous machinery—and then drowsiness can cause serious accidents). Some antibiotics, like penicillin, that have been around for decades, battle bacterial infections well, but can cause mild-to-life-threatening allergic reactions. Other antibiotics, like tetracycline, help people who can't take penicillin, but these drugs often cause stomach or intestinal discomfort. Even common household aspirin can irritate your stomach lining. Worse yet, aspirin has been known to trigger **Reye's syndrome** when given to children battling chicken pox, influenza, or other viral infections. These side effects may occur even when users are exactly following the manufacturer's instructions for use (which is not the case when OTC drugs are abused).

All these side effects are considered adverse reactions, whether mild or severe, and most were observed in clinical trials before the FDA approved each drug. The FDA weighed the drug's effectiveness and its potential to do good against its potential to do harm. The potential for abuse is one of the factors weighed by the FDA before each medication is approved for public use. Approval doesn't mean that the drugs are harmless—they still might cause adverse reactions, and they can still be abused. To make sure that prescribing physicians and the public know about potential adverse reactions, the FDA requires manufacturers to tell them of both the benefits and the risks of any new drug they want to sell.

Weight-loss aids and other potentially harmful dietary supplements are not considered drugs under FDA guidelines. Instead, they are categorized as food, which means that they are not subject to the same types of regulations as drugs. Unlike drugs, they are not allowed to claim that they cure, treat, or prevent a disease or illness, but they can inform consumers how ingredients contained in them can affect organs or processes, or that there are relationships between its ingredients and lowering the risk of a disease. However, the FDA does not regulate whether or not a dietary supplement is safe and effective, or the quality of the ingredients used. The only time a manufacturer must notify the FDA that they intend to produce a supplement is when its product contains a new dietary ingredient.

3 Who Uses Over-the-Counter Drugs?

Most drugs that are subject to abuse have a typical user *profile*. In the case of OTC drugs, teenagers in high school and even middle school are the group that is most likely to engage in abuse. Studies have shown that the largest increases in abuse are committed by people between the ages of thirteen and sixteen. OTC drugs are especially popular in dance clubs and raves, where they are used as an alternative to the more traditional drug of choice, ecstasy. This increase in abuse is being reflected by national data. The American Association of Poison Control Centers reported that between 2000 and 2003, poison center calls related to teenage DXM abuse rose from 1,623 to 3,271. In that same time period, calls from other age groups rose only from 900 to 1,111.

OTC drugs are readily available to teenagers. They're legal—and they are cheap.

Choosing OTC Drugs Over Others

OTC drugs have a lot of pluses in the minds of some abusers, leading them to decide on OTC drugs as their drug of choice. The biggest draw is that OTC drugs are not illegal. Users are able to simply walk or drive to the store, pick up a pack of cough medicine, and take it home. It's much easier and safer to legally buy a drug in a supermarket than to **clandestinely** buy an illegal drug through a drug dealer.

Users, especially teenagers, also take OTC drugs because they are cheap. These users can get high for a few dollars, unlike the hundreds of dollars required to buy a steady supply of similar illegal drugs. DXM has been compared to ecstasy, ketamine, and PCP, producing the same hallucinogenic effects that these drugs are famed for, but for a lot less money. If users can experience ultimately the same thing with DXM as with illegal drugs, they predictably choose the drug that costs the least. This helps to explain why teenagers are the age group most likely to abuse OTC drugs. Without full-time jobs, teenagers don't have a lot of money to spend on recreational drug use, so they turn to the cheapest alternatives.

Because OTC drugs are not illegal, at least not yet, teenagers view them less seriously than their more famous counterparts. They see commercials for them every day, and have probably already taken them to relieve pain or cold symptoms. Taking the extra step and ingesting larger amounts of those same drugs doesn't seem like such a big deal. The pill or syrup forms of OTC drugs are also more familiar to teenagers and, in safe amounts, are *condoned* by their parents. Additionally, while some people might be squeamish of injecting a drug, using a syringe, or snorting a powder, taking a pill or swallowing syrup seems safe and easy.

The relative novelty of OTC drug abuse and the more widespread abuse of other, illegal drugs means that the

A Parent's Guide to Preventing Teen Cough Medicine Abuse, published by the Partnership for a Drug-Free America, suggests these steps for parents who want to communicate with teens about OTC drugs:

- Be clear that you do not want your teen taking medicine without your knowledge.
- Teach your teens and younger children to respect medicines. Medicines are important tools in healthcare, but they must be used according to directions.
- Make sure your teen understands that abusing cough medicine—just as abusing illegal drugs—can be very dangerous.

Is there anything you would add to this list?

average person has little knowledge of it; some people are not even aware that there is a problem at all. Because of this, teenagers may not be knowledgeable about the consequences of their abuse. School health classes often don't

Teenagers like to do things in groups. They like to dress alike, talk alike, act alike. That may be one reason why OTC abuse occurs in "pockets" within schools and neighborhoods.

The Partnership for a Drug-Free America conducted a survey in 2005 to gather data concerning OTC drug abuse. Among other things, the study concluded:

- Ten percent of all high school students had abused cough medicine.
- Fifty-five percent of teenagers don't think that getting high off cough medicine is risky.
- Only one-third of parents have discussed OTC drug abuse with their children.
- The Internet is the main source of information on OTC drug use.

include OTC drugs in their discussions of abuse of other, more common drugs like marijuana, nor have there been commercials on TV warning against OTC drug abuse. If parents have never heard of OTC drug abuse, they can't warn their children about its dangers. Without being exposed to information regarding the dangers of drugs like DXM, users may not be aware of how risky those drugs truly are.

Reasons for Drug Abuse

Usually, teenagers don't simply open up the medicine cabinet and take a few pills on a whim. There are underlying reasons behind why they start abusing any type of drug, including over-the-counter medications. The high intensity of the lives of many of today's teenagers is one of the causes of drug abuse. Teens cite stress as one of the major reasons for their drug use: drugs offer them a chance to escape from the daily stress they experience due to school, friends, or family.

DXM abuse can cause unpleasant sensations that include nausea, headaches, and frightening hallucinations.

Researchers have found that some people, especially some teenagers, are more likely to abuse drugs than others. Family history has a large part in predicting whether or not an individual will become addicted to drugs. Other environmental factors also come in to play. Youths who feel they don't fit in, have little self-confidence, and who have depression are more likely to start abusing drugs.

Children who don't learn about the dangers of drugs at home are also more likely to do drugs. According to the Partnership for a Drug-Free America, children who have talked to their parents or other family members about drugs are 50 percent less likely to start abusing them later in life. If people are taught early on from supportive people they trust that drugs are dangerous, they will likely come to understand that doing drugs is a risky decision.

DXM Abuse

According to law enforcement data, DXM abuse occurs in small pockets. As one teenager discovers cold medicine's potential for abuse, most likely from the Internet, he or she spreads the word to friends and fellow students. In 2003, for example, Collier County, Florida, witnessed an outbreak of DXM abuse. In September, a thirteen-year-old girl brought Coricidin Cough and Cold medicine to her middle school. She gave five tablets each to six friends; three had to be hospitalized later that day. In November, a high school boy distributed Coricidin Cough and Cold pills to three girls. One of them had to be flown to a hospital.

Abuse isn't limited to one area of the country or continent, because information about abuse is usually spread over the Internet. Anyone in the world with Internet access can learn about DXM. Besides in the United States and Canada, abuse of DXM has been reported in countries such as Germany, Sweden, and Australia.

The extent to which DXM is abused is a complicated situation. The same reasons that people choose to abuse DXM can also be the same reasons that others choose not to. The fact that cough medicines and other OTC drugs are so familiar turns some people off from using them to get high. They don't view drinking an entire bottle of cough syrup, something they may take occasionally anyway for medicinal purposes, as appealing. Other people are skeptical as to whether they really can get high off of DXM. Abusing and getting high off familiar medicinal drugs is not a concept that all people are willing to accept.

Since DXM abuse has not generally been mentioned in school or in advertising, people who are not aware of the problem remain unaware. This is harmful for those who choose to abuse DXM without knowing the consequences, but it also helps to keep in check the basic knowledge that cough medicines can in fact be abused. If teenagers don't know that they can get high off of cough medicines, pain relievers, and allergy medications, they aren't likely to open up the medicine cabinet and abuse them.

Another important reason that DXM abuse is not more widespread is that not everyone who tries to get high off it enjoys it. Many people who do try remember it as a bad experience that isn't worth repeating. They find that the negative effects of DXM, such as nausea, headaches, and itching, are a disincentive to continue to use cough products to get high. Other people are frightened

Many teenage girls aspire to extreme thinness. In many cases, this goal may not be realistic or even healthy, depending on the young woman's body type. Living in a culture that values thinness, however, makes adolescent girls particularly vulnerable to the claims of the diet pill industry.

Mona Lisa, the woman in Leonardo da Vinci's famous masterpiece, was once considered to be a standard for feminine beauty—and yet in today's world, her plump face and round shoulders might make her turn to diet pills in order to trim down!

64   Chapter 3—Who Uses Over-the-Counter Drugs?

by extreme hallucinations, which can include hallucinations of death. Information gathered from abusers' experiences suggests that only about one-third who try to get high off DXM actually enjoy it.

Recognizing DXM Abuse

There are many warning signs that can be used by parents, friends, and school officials to determine if someone they know is abusing DXM. Signs that indicate a teenager is using any drugs include dropping grades, a change in friends, loss of interest in usual activities, a change in behavior, stealing money, and/or a change in appearance or weight. DXM-specific indications include clues such as empty or disappearing containers of medicine from cupboards or the presence of large quantities of cough medicine in a teen's bedroom. He or she may also be visiting DXM Web sites in order to learn how to get high.

Diet Pills and Teenage Girls

Adolescent girls (as well as older women) are the group most vulnerable to the advertising claims of diet pills and other OTC products claiming to reduce weight. Our culture tells girls that being "pretty" is often more important than being smart or healthy or kind. In desperate attempts to conform to the cultural definition of prettiness, girls may turn to OTC products. This emphasis on physical appearance is one of the major distortions of our society. It fails to recognize that other qualities are far more essential to both an individual's personhood and the entire culture's well-being. What's more, cultural definitions of beauty are variable, depending on many factors.

Historically, beauty standards have often been set by the upper classes in a society. In many cultures, physical **attributes** that are associated with wealth also become associated with beauty. For example, in societies that are experiencing famine or lack of food, a plump body (a sign of wealth and strength in an otherwise bleak picture of wasting and emaciation) is often seen as beautiful. In a society that has plenty of food (like North America), thinness becomes associated with wealth because wealthy people have the time and the money to dedicate to things like fitness and special diets. In such a well-fed society, being thin or skinny becomes beautiful. In situations like these, people do not necessarily consciously associate the physical attributes of wealth with beauty, but wealth is desirable, and therefore the physical attributes of wealthy people become desirable. Similarly, in societies where large families consisting of many children are desirable, physical attributes that are associated with fertility, like wide hips and large breasts in women, are also associated with beauty. In societies where few children are desired, these physical signs of fertility may not be considered beautiful. These trends are of course not universal, but there are many examples throughout history of beauty being associated with wealth and good health.

A good way to see how images of beauty have changed throughout time is to look at art. Artwork often portrays **idealized** images of the period in which the art was created. When you look at paintings depicting Greek gods

The average supermodel is five feet, eleven inches tall, weighs 117 pounds, wears a size four, and is thinner than 98 percent of American women. The average American woman is five feet, four inches tall and weighs 142 pounds.

Many North American girls and women find themselves in a constant (and often unhealthy) battle to be thin.

Abusing Over-the-Counter Drugs 67

The "ideal" feminine shape is largely a myth that few real women can achieve.

and goddesses, for example, you may be surprised to see how round and plump the women are. Renaissance women were also portrayed with round bellies and wide hips. In the 1920s' Art Deco period, slim, boyish women are often portrayed.

In today's world, the media—television, radio, movies, the Internet, newspapers, and magazines—are like the circulatory system that carries cultural "blood" to all parts of our society. A good deal of the messages that are pumped through the popular media have to do with selling products that promise to make young women more beautiful. But in order to sell you a beauty product, a company must be sure that the buyers' ideal or conception of beauty is the same image that the product promises to bestow. For example, if in a certain place people dislike plump abdomens, then it makes sense for a company to advertise products that promise to reduce the size of a person's abdomen. However, if everyone in a certain place liked plump abdomens, it would be ridiculous for a company to try to sell products meant to slim everyone's stomach down, because no one would buy the product and the company would lose money.

To be sure that their products are desirable to the population, companies will on the one hand study society for trends and then develop products that are compatible with those trends. On the other hand, however, companies themselves also try to create trends and to keep profitable trends going by promoting certain ideas over others and trying to get you to believe their ideas are good ones. Companies have many tactics for persuading you into thinking a particular idea, image, or product is the "right" one and worth spending your money on. Often these tactics consist of using actresses, models, sports heroes, and other people who *exude* images of health, physical strength, and beauty to *endorse* products. Advertisements involving such people imply that by using the product, you can become like the person who is endorsing the product. In the vast majority of cases, however, the famous or beautiful people you see never even used the product they are endorsing before they were offered money to endorse it!

North American Women: Battling to Be Thin

Walk down the checkout aisle at the grocery story. Turn on the television for ten minutes. Flip through a fashion magazine, or look at the advertisements hanging in storefronts. It's pretty clear what a beautiful North American young woman is supposed to look like. She's supposed to be tall and thin with perfect skin, voluptuous breasts, and long, flowing hair. But how many women do you know who actually look like this? The truth is that the female body you see on the front of that fashion magazine is an *unattainable* ideal. You may think that woman is simply blessed with rare *genes*. She probably is, but her beauty secret goes much further than that. She also has the benefit of dieticians, personal trainers, and makeup artists. Her job is to look good, so a huge portion of her time (and a great deal of money) is devoted to developing this image. Even with all this help, however, this woman will still never look as good walking down the street as she does on the cover of the magazine. That's because her beauty is not just the product of good genes, starvation, hard work, and talented artists. She has also been photographed under special lights and carefully planned conditions. After that photograph was taken, it went through an elaborate design process that included airbrushing and computer enhancement to minimize or eliminate any re-maining "flaws" and to "improve" parts of the body. Like so much of what you will read inside that magazine, the picture on its cover is a work of fiction.

The look many women struggle so hard to obtain is unrealistic. All over North America, women and girls hate their bodies and spend a great amount of money try-ing to achieve something that only exists in pictures. The abuse of OTC drugs are just one of the dangers to which they may be vulnerable—but this is nevertheless a very real and *potent* danger.

4 What are the Dangers of Over-the-Counter Drugs?

Like all other drugs that are abused, users get more than they bargained for when taking OTC drugs. Besides inducing hallucinations, relieving stress, or helping with weight loss, OTC drugs have a host of both short- and long-term side effects that are anything but fun or beneficial.

DXM

Abusing DXM leads to many physical side effects that are at the least uncomfortable, and at the most extreme, possibly deadly. Some of the milder effects that an abuser may experience include dizziness, nausea, a loss of co-ordination, sweating, blurred vision and dilated pupils, slurred speech, headaches, skin sensitivity, redness in the face, dry skin and mouth, and numbness in the *extremities*. The body's muscles are also adversely affected, and

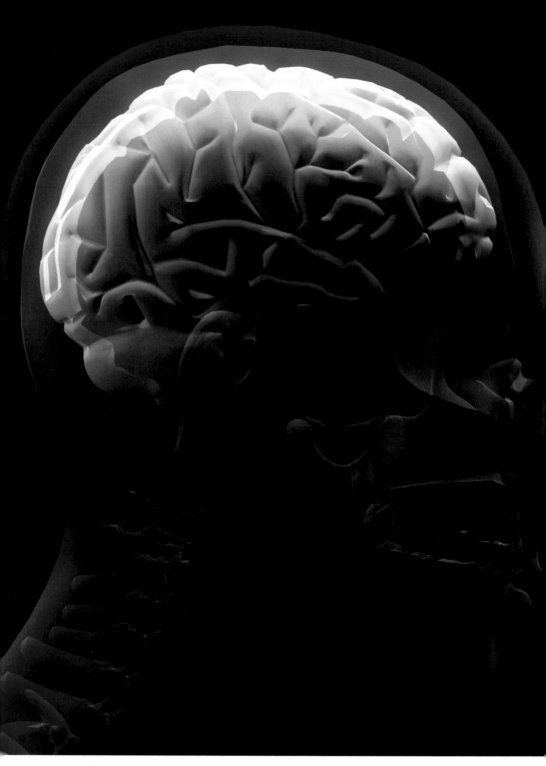

DXM contains chemicals that affect the way the brain functions. Abusing this medication can cause confusion, paranoia, and other distorted perceptions.

tremors or involuntary twitching can appear in those high on DXM. Another frequent side effect is called robo itch. Abusers sometimes feel an intense itching sensation that is caused by the release of **histamines** in the body. Many of these signs are visible, and can be used to identify someone who is high on DXM.

Not all of DXM's side effects are physical. Since it is a substance that works on the brain, users experience several adverse psychological side effects too. Ironically (since people generally abuse DXM in an effort to get "high"), dysphoria—extreme sadness—can occur, along with **paranoia**, confusion, **disorientation**, distorted time perception, and **mania**. It is these feelings that lead to some people's "bad trips," frightening and painful experiences that can occur while high on DXM.

DXM abuse can also lead to more serious dangers. The body temperature can rise, the heart starts to beat irregularly or at a faster rate (called tachycardia), blood pressure rises, and the user may lose consciousness. Death is also a very real possibility. While deaths related purely to DXM itself are rare, they do occur. A well-covered story in 2005 documented the deaths of five men who abused DXM, leading to the arrest of two other men who sold them the drug over the Internet. More common are deaths that happen when DXM is being used along with alcohol or another drug.

While the short-term effects of abusing DXM may be obvious, the long-term ones are not. Not enough research has been done on DXM abuse to reach a conclusion about whether or not DXM can harm a person irreparably. However, according to the little research that has been conducted and the abusers themselves, abuse of DXM over a long period of time may cause learning problems and memory impairment. With the growing knowledge of OTC drug abuse, more research will be conducted into its long-term effects, and the whole story of this drug's dangers will eventually unfold.

Impaired Judgment: Hidden Dangers

People use DXM in order to experience the feeling of being high. However, this sensation brings with it a loss of judgment and motor skills. This makes the user not only dangerous to herself but to others as well. People are used to hearing about drunk drivers and the accidents and sorrow they cause, but they seldom connect these tragedies to something as seemingly harmless as cold medicine. However, the same types of tragic situations can occur if a person is high on any drug, including DXM or other OTC drugs. Because a person lacks the ability to make quick, intelligent decisions, as well as appropriate motor skills necessary for operating a motor vehicle, choosing to drive while high is very risky.

Other activities are dangerous as well. Swimming while high on an OTC drug can be deadly. The confusion and lack of coordination brought on by DXM can lead to drowning. Even simple activities can become risky as well. In Colorado in 2003, a fourteen-year-old boy was hit by two cars and died while crossing the street. He was high on DXM and was most likely unable to correctly judge how fast and how close the cars were.

Being high on DXM may cause some people to become violent. These people are especially dangerous, since they are unable to control their violence and judge their actions. Even normally docile people can become violent under the influence of drugs. When they are unaccountable for their actions, they pose a threat not only to themselves but also to other people who may be unconnected to the abuser.

Using any drug while swimming can be a deadly combination.

Combining alcohol with DXM makes both drugs far more dangerous.

Even More Dangerous in Combination

DXM abuse is harmful enough on its own, but the cold medicines that contain it also sometimes contain other products that can heighten the danger of abusing them. For example, several cough syrups with DXM in them also contain acetaminophen, a pain reliever. Taking large doses of it causes liver damage, strokes, heart attacks, and death. Even if abusers are familiar with the dangers of DXM itself, they might not be aware that other substances included in their drug are just as harmful. They

MAOI and SSRI are acronyms for two types of antidepression medication. MAOI stands for monoamine oxidase inhibitor. MAOIs must be prescribed and used with caution because they tend to dangerously interact with other types of drugs. Today, other forms of antidepressants are usually prescribed for depression patients first. If those medicines do not work, MAOIs are sometimes used with caution. People taking MAOIs have to restrict their diets and watch what other drugs and medicines they take in order to prevent interactions. SSRI, an antidepressant that is more commonly used, stands for selective serotonin reuptake inhibitor. They are generally able to be tolerated by more people and can be used for more minor depressive illnesses.

not only have to deal with the damaging side effects of that particular drug, but also those of any other substance that may be included in the medicine they take.

Taking DXM in conjunction with other drugs or alcohol is much more dangerous than taking DXM alone. In fact, most emergency room visits relating to DXM involve other drugs or alcohol. For example, if DXM is taken with ecstasy, the abuser is at risk for hyperthermia, a dramatic rise in body temperature that can be fatal. This is fairly common, since dealers selling ecstasy have been known to include the cheaper DXM in their product, making the buyer unaware that he is mixing two drugs. Abusing more than one type of substance at one time creates a *synergistic* effect: in other words, the effects of both drugs are increased when used together, becoming more potent than either of them when taken alone.

Taking DXM with other OTC drugs can also be risky, even if taken at medicinal levels. People taking monoamine oxidase inhibitors (MAOIs) or selective serotonin reuptake inhibitors (SSRIs) along with products containing DXM could be in danger. Using DXM, even at medicinal levels, up to two weeks after stopping one of these drugs can be harmful.

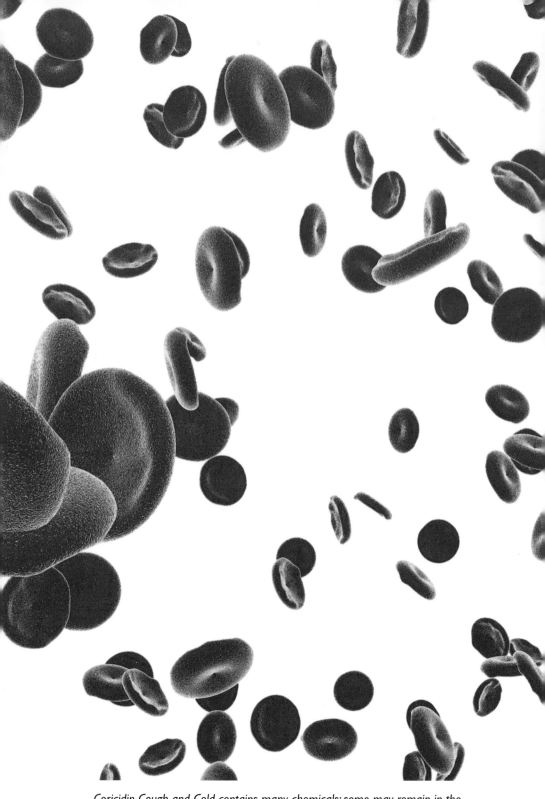

Coricidin Cough and Cold contains many chemicals; some may remain in the bloodstream long after others, causing potential dangers to the body.

Taking both at the same time could cause fevers, heart problems, *hypertension*, and death.

Coricidin Cough and Cold

Coricidin Cough and Cold is one of the most dangerous of the DXM-containing medications. Not only does it contain more DXM per unit of medicine than most other cough relievers, it also contains chlorpheniramine maleate—a dangerous secondary ingredient—and acetaminophen. Taking high doses of Coricidin Cough and Cold, and therefore chlorpheniramine maleate can cause seizures, bleeding, breathing problems, loss of consciousness, and death.

Because Coricidin Cough and Cold contains so many different types of substances in one pill, the body isn't able to process them all at once. While the body uses up some of each type of medicine, some remains present in the bloodstream, where it can be harmful to the body. For some people, who usually do not know who they are beforehand, it is even more difficult for their bodies to absorb and *metabolize* these substances. For these individuals, taking Coricidin Cough and Cold is especially dangerous, since they are more susceptible to the medicine's harmful side effects. Unfortunately, their inability to process the drug often remains unknown until they abuse the cough medication. By then, it is too late to avoid the nausea, loss of consciousness, or other negative effects that the extra drugs in their body cause. Estimates say that about 10 percent of Caucasians have this problem.

Just as Harmful as Its Illegal Cousins

Just like users of the more famous illegal drugs, DXM abusers can experience both tolerance and withdrawal symptoms. Tolerance occurs when users' bodies become accustomed to the drug that is being put into it. Users report that as time goes on and abuse continues, the user needs to use more and more DXM in order to get the same level of euphoria and disassociation she experienced at the beginning of her abuse.

Although studies have not conclusively proved that abusers can go through DXM withdrawal, many reports from actual abusers suggest that it can happen after a long period of taking the drug. Withdrawal occurs when addicts cease taking a drug, and the body and mind, which have become dependent on that drug, react to the sudden change. They may experience symptoms like muscle aches, insomnia, diarrhea, vomiting, weight loss, and goose bumps. Psychologically, people withdrawing from DXM will feel anxiety, restlessness, and depression.

Antihistamines and Sleep Aids

Antihistamines, used to treat allergies, can cause some side effects, like drowsiness, dizziness, nervousness, mild euphoria, and tremors, even when used medicinally at suggested doses. Abusers who take many times the recommended amount experience more intense side effects. Along with the enhanced euphoria they are looking for, the other side effects are also increased. Additionally, muscle spasms, irregular heartbeat, faintness, and convulsions can also occur with extremely high levels of antihistamines.

Not surprisingly, people who abuse sleep aids to get high end up having problems with their sleep cycles. Sleep aids, as they promise, cause drowsiness. When abused during the day, obvious problems arise. Normal

Abusing sleep aids can interfere with normal sleep cycles, causing wakefulness at night—and sleepiness during the day when you should be alert for school or work.

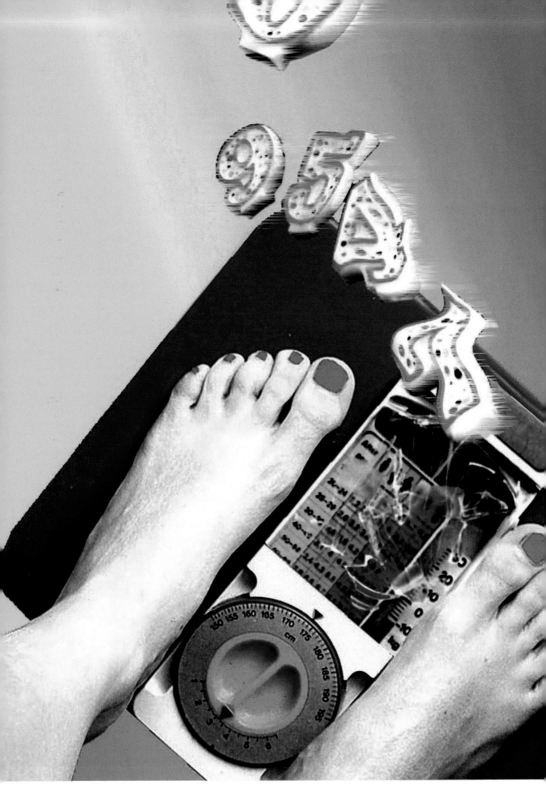

Using a dietary supplement to lose weight may have dangerous side effects.

patterns of sleep during the night and wakefulness during the day are necessary for normal functioning of the human body. Interfering with sleep patterns can lead to other problems, such as mood changes and falling asleep while operating machinery or performing other daily chores that suddenly

Narcolepsy is a neurological disorder. People with narcolepsy have problems with their sleep cycle and are subject to suddenly falling asleep throughout the day. Other symptoms of narcolepsy include hallucinations and temporary paralysis.

become dangerous. According to some studies, extended use of this type of OTC drug, and experiencing the accompanying tiredness, can even lead to narcolepsy.

Weight-Loss Solutions and Other Dietary Supplements

Ingredients included in weight-loss aids or other dietary supplements can be unsafe, even though the packaging may say that the product is "all-natural." Just because a product claims to be made only of natural materials does not mean that it is automatically safe to use. Some substances found in nature are toxic to humans and should not be ingested. For a famous example, simply consider marijuana: a naturally growing plant, but an illegal drug that can cause health problems nonetheless. One of the "natural" ingredients that can be found in weight-loss aids is bitter orange, which contains a stimulant that is chemically similar to ephedrine and may also have the same side effects. Other ingredients, such as usnic acid that may cause liver damage or aristolochic acid that may

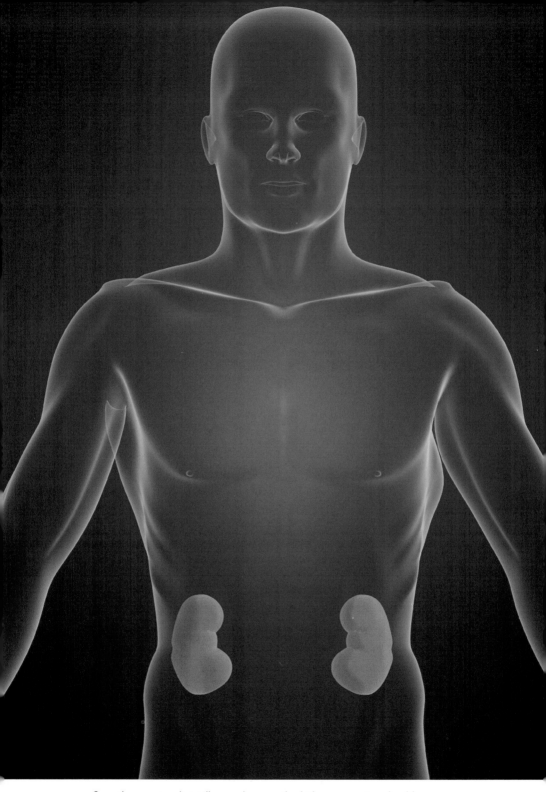

*Over-the-counter diet pills can damage the kidneys, a serious health conse-
quence that can make dialysis or kidney transplant necessary to avoid death.*

Electrolytes are important minerals that are required for normal functioning of the body. They are found in the bloodstream, as well as in other bodily fluids such as sweat. It is necessary to maintain normal levels of electrolytes such as sodium, potassium, and bicarbonate in order to sustain muscle functioning, nerve impulses, and normal fluid levels in the body. When laxatives and diuretics are used, water and electrolytes are removed from the body, causing an electrolyte imbalance and accompanying health problems.

cause kidney damage, can harm internal organs. Taking fen-phen, or fenfluramine, may result in diarrhea, chest pain, and high blood pressure, not the sought-after weight loss.

People who abuse ipecac syrup in order to lose weight are at risk for cardiac problems, including chest pain, irregular or rapid heartbeat, and heart attacks. Respiratory problems also occur, along with seizures and hemorrhaging. Laxatives, another medicine subject to abuse in hope of losing weight, are also harmful if taken in excess. Short-term effects include dehydration and electrolyte imbalances, while long-term effects can consist of permanent bowel damage and death. The lack of water and other nutrients in the body can damage the kidneys and lead to kidney stones or kidney failure, which can require kidney dialysis and possibly the need for a kidney transplant. Diuretics, or water pills, also cause dehydration and electrolyte imbalances if abused and have similar long-term effects on the kidneys.

Because OTC drugs are legal, abusers may consider them safer—but clearly, this not necessarily so. As more research is done on their potential for abuse, new and stricter legal restrictions may come into play as well.

5 Treatment

Coming off of any dependency or addiction is not easy and should not be done on one's own. The guidance of a health-care professional can prevent or lessen withdrawal symptoms; the physical toll on the body is not as extreme as it could be. DXM withdrawal symptoms can include:

- restlessness
- depression (which may be severe)
- muscle and bone pain
- insomnia
- diarrhea
- vomiting
- cold flashes with goose bumps

Though most experts consider these withdrawal symptoms to be mild (and they are, compared to the withdrawal symptoms of some drugs), to the person undergoing them, the discomfort can be intense. Some experts believe the best way to come off of DXM and other OTC drugs is to do so "cold turkey," that is, to stop taking them completely at once. Others suggest that increasingly lower doses of DXM be given until the individual is weaned off the medication.

Regardless of how one ends his relationship with DXM, a new way of living must be learned. The first step in this new life plan, and in overcoming addiction to DXM and other OTC medications, is the same as with every other form of addiction: admit there is a problem, that one is an addict. In some ways, this may be one of the hardest of a series of incredibly hard steps. But it is impossible to finish the journey to sobriety without taking that first step of admitting to being an addict.

The most effective method of addiction treatment involves a multidisciplinary approach—and it doesn't happen over night.

Detoxification

When one decides to break free from addiction, the body must go through a process of withdrawal to rid itself of the toxic substances of the drug. Through a process called detoxification, the individual goes through some or all of the withdrawal symptoms listed earlier in this chapter. How long withdrawal lasts can depend on how much, how often, and what type of OTC drug was taken. For those addicted to OTC drugs, the detoxification process generally takes place at home, although hospitalization may be required in some cases.

For someone who is mildly dependent on OTC medications, this process might be enough to prevent further misuse. The person who is more seriously addicted to OTC drugs, however, needs follow-up treatment; studies

Tackling an addiction is often long, slow work.

Support groups offer emotional and social help when a person is recovering from a drug problem. Celebrating the victories is an important part of that.

have shown that most people with addictions will return to their previous behaviors if treatment ends with detoxification. There are two primary methods of treating addiction: behavioral and *pharmacological*.

Behavioral Treatment Programs

The most common treatment plan for OTC drug abuse is participation in a behavioral treatment program. Put simply, behavioral treatment programs teach people with addictions to change their behaviors so they are less likely to repeat those that led to addiction in the first place. Unfortunately, nothing about addiction is simple. Though behavioral treatment programs do help those with addictions find ways to avoid behaviors that can cause a relapse, they also need to help them discover what led to those behaviors initially. Cognitive-behavioral therapy helps the individuals recognize how thought patterns influence behaviors. With therapy, individuals learn how to change negative thought patterns, thereby changing behaviors. Individual and family therapy can help the person with addiction and those around her learn how to live with and as a recovering addict. Therapy can also help the addicted individual and her associates handle relapses since most people do relapse at some point during recovery.

Behavioral treatment programs also help those with addictions handle life without the OTC medication, including the depression that sometimes comes with quitting the drug.

One reason individuals begin to abuse OTC medications is their availability. It is highly likely that the recovering abuser will have to come face-to-face with his drug of choice at some point in the future. After all, these

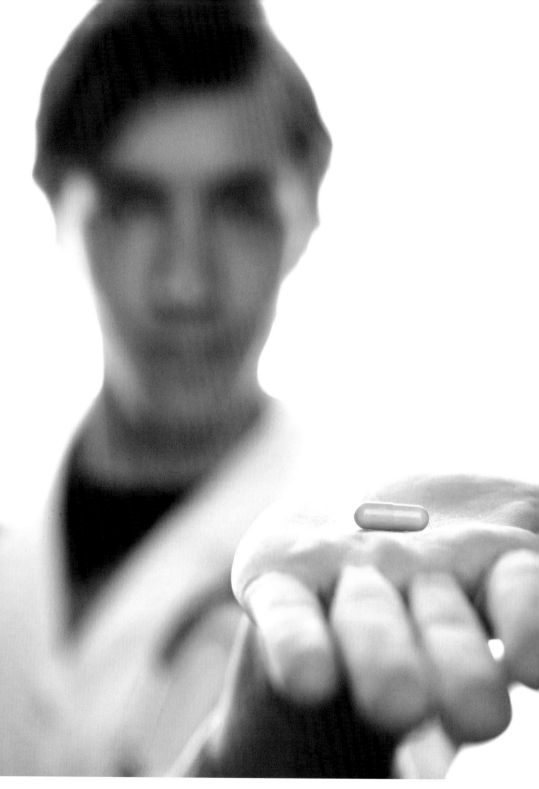

No magic pill exists to cure dependence on DXM.

are legitimate medications for which there is a recognized medical purpose. These individuals may also have the need for such medications at some time. Behavioral treatment programs will help such individuals learn to deal with that issue as well.

In general, behavioral treatment programs often begin with a period of inpatient treatment. Depending on the length, severity, and drug of addiction, inpatient treatment can be short-term (usually a minimum of thirty days) or long-term residential. At first, some programs allow inpatients to have minimal—if any—contact with the "outside world." They concentrate on learning about themselves and their relationship with the drug. Later, family and perhaps close friends are encouraged to participate in the treatment program.

Pharmacological Treatment Programs

Medications have proven to be effective in treating addiction to many drugs. They are used in both inpatient and outpatient settings. Although such treatment protocol is beneficial to many, for someone addicted to DXM or other OTC medications, it is probably not the best option.

Most treatment programs use a combination of behavioral treatment and pharmacological methods. Individuals are also encouraged to supplement their programs with support groups such as Narcotics Anonymous.

Narcotics Anonymous

Based on the twelve-step program of Alcoholics Anonymous (AA), Narcotics Anonymous (NA) helps those addicted to prescription painkillers stay sober in the outside world. The first NA meetings were held in the early 1950s in Los Angeles, California. As found on its Web site (www.na.org), the organization described itself this way in its first publication:

> NA is a nonprofit fellowship or society of men and women for whom drugs had become a major problem. We . . . meet regularly to help each other stay clean. . . . We are not interested in what or how much you used . . . but only in what you want to do about your problem and how we can help.

In the more than fifty years since, NA has grown into one of the largest organizations of its kind. Today, groups are located all over the world, and its books and pamphlets are published in thirty-two languages. No matter where the group is located, each chapter is based on the twelve steps first formulated in AA:

1. We admitted we were powerless over drugs—that our lives had become unmanageable.
2. Came to believe that a Power greater than ourselves could restore us to sanity.
3. Made a decision to turn our will and our lives over to the care of God as we understand Him.
4. Made a searching and fearless moral inventory of ourselves.
5. Admitted to God, and to ourselves, and to another human being the exact nature of our wrongs.
6. We're entirely ready to have God remove all these defects of character.
7. Humbly asked Him to remove our shortcomings.

According to NA's beliefs, reliance on a "Higher Power" can play an important role in recovery from drug dependence.

Abusing Over-the-Counter Drugs 97

Each individual is different. This means that no single treatment for drug depen-dence will work with all people. Treatment approaches need to be designed and adapted to meet individual needs.

8. Made a list of all persons we had harmed, and became willing to make amends to them all.
9. Made direct amends to such people wherever possible, except when to do so would injure them or others.
10. Continued to take personal inventory and when we were wrong promptly admitted it.
11. Sought through prayer and meditation to improve our conscious contact with God as we understand Him, praying only for knowledge of His will for us and the power to carry that out.
12. Having had a spiritual awakening as the result of these steps, we tried to carry this message to drug addicts and to practice these principles in all our affairs.

Though attendance at and participation in NA meetings will not guarantee a recovery free from temptation and relapse, they can play an important role in staying sober.

Principles of Treatment

The NIDA has come up with a list of thirteen principles that make up a good treatment program. These include:

1. *No single treatment is appropriate for all individuals.* Matching treatment settings, interventions, and services to each individual's particular problems and needs is critical to his or her ultimate success in returning to productive functioning in the family, workplace, and society.

2. *Treatment needs to be readily available.* Because individuals who are addicted to drugs may be uncertain about

entering treatment, taking advantage of opportunities when they are ready for treatment is crucial. Potential treatment applicants can be lost if treatment is not immediately available or is not readily accessible.

3. *Effective treatment attends to multiple needs of the individual, not just his or her drug use.* To be effective, treatment must address the individual's drug use and any associated medical, psychological, social, vocational, and legal problems.

4. *An individual's treatment and services plan must be assessed continually and modified as necessary to ensure that the plan meets the person's changing needs.* A patient may require varying combinations of services and treatment components during the course of treatment and recovery. In addition to counseling or psychotherapy, a patient at times may require medication, other medical services, family therapy, parenting instruction, vocational rehabilitation, and social and legal services. It is critical that the treatment approach be appropriate to the individual's age, gender, ethnicity, and culture.

5. *Remaining in treatment for an adequate period of time is critical for treatment effectiveness.* The appropriate duration for an individual depends on his or her problems and needs. Research indicates that for most patients, the threshold of significant improvement is reached at about three months in treatment. After this threshold is reached, additional treatment can produce further progress toward recovery. Because people often leave treatment prematurely, programs should include strategies to engage and keep patients in treatment.

Treatment for drug problems must include all parts of an individual's life, including her emotional problems, as these can contribute to her drug habit.

Although there is no medication that cures drug abuse, many individuals who abuse drugs also have psychiatric disorders such as depression or anxiety— and if these issues are addressed with prescription drugs, individuals will be better able to tackle their drug dependency.

6. *Counseling (individual and/or group) and other behavioral therapies are critical components of effective treatment for addiction.* In therapy, patients address issues of motivation, build skills to resist drug use, replace drug-using activities with constructive and rewarding nondrug-using activities, and improve problem-solving abilities. Behavioral therapy also facilitates interpersonal relationships and the individual's ability to function in the family and community.

7. *Medications are an important element of treatment for many patients, especially when combined with counseling and other behavioral therapies.* For patients with mental disorders who have used an illegal drug to self-medicate, both behavioral treatments and medications can be critically important.

8. *Addicted or drug-abusing individuals with coexisting mental disorders should have both disorders treated in an integrated way.* Because addictive disorders and mental disorders often occur in the same individual, patients presenting for either condition should be assessed and treated for the co-occurrence of the other type of disorder.

9. *Medical detoxification is only the first stage of addiction treatment and by itself does little to change long-term drug use.* Medical detoxification safely manages the acute physical symptoms of withdrawal associated with stopping drug use. While detoxification alone is rarely sufficient to help addicts achieve long-term abstinence, for some individuals it is a strongly indicated precursor to effective drug addiction treatment.

10. *Treatment does not need to be voluntary to be effective.* Strong motivation can facilitate the treatment process, however. Sanctions or enticements in the family, employment setting, or criminal justice system can increase significantly both treatment entry and retention rates and the success of drug treatment interventions.

11. *Possible drug use during treatment must be monitored continuously.* Lapses to drug use can occur during treatment. The objective monitoring of a patient's drug and alcohol use during treatment, such as through urinalysis or other tests, can help the patient withstand urges to use drugs. Such monitoring also can provide early evidence of drug use so that the individual's treatment plan can be adjusted. Feedback to patients who test positive for illicit drug use is an important element of monitoring.

12. *Treatment programs should provide assessment for HIV/AIDS, hepatitis B and C, tuberculosis and other infectious diseases, and counseling to help patients modify or change behaviors that place themselves or others at risk of infection.* Counseling can help patients avoid high-risk behavior. Counseling also can help people who are already infected manage their illness.

13. *Recovery from drug addiction can be a long-term process and frequently requires multiple episodes of treatment.* As with other chronic illnesses, relapses to drug use can occur during or after successful treatment episodes. Addicted individuals may require prolonged treatment and multiple episodes of treatment to achieve long-term abstinence and fully restored functioning.

Recovery from drug dependency is sometimes a long process, with many ups and downs along the way. Relapses along the way are considered normal, but the ultimate goal is a drug-free life.

What Do Rehab Programs Accomplish?

Abstinence

In many cases it seems that as long as the substance is in the bloodstream, thinking remains distorted. Often during the first days or weeks of total abstinence, we see a gradual clearing of thinking processes. This is a complex psychological and biological phenomenon, and is one of the elements that inpatient programs are able to provide by making sure the patient is fully detoxified and remains abstinent during his or her stay.

Removal of Denial

In some cases, when someone other than the patient, such as a parent, employer, or other authority, is convinced there is a problem, but the addict is not yet sure, voluntary attendance at a rehab program will provide enough clarification to remove this basic denial. Even those who are convinced they have a problem with substances usually don't admit to themselves or others the full extent of the addiction. Rehab uses group process to identify and help the individual to let go of these expectable forms of denial.

Removal of Isolation

As addictions progress, relationships deteriorate in quality. However, the bonds between fellow recovering people are widely recognized as one of the few forces powerful enough to keep recovery on track. The rehab experience, whether it is inpatient or outpatient, involves in-depth sharing in a group setting. This kind of sharing creates strong interpersonal bonds among group members. These bonds help to form a support system that will be powerful enough to sustain the individual during the first months of abstinence.

"Basic Training"

Basic training is a good way to think of the experience of rehab. Soldiers need a rapid course to give them the basic knowledge and skills they will need to fight in a war. Some kinds of learning need to be practiced so well that you can do them without thinking. In addition to the learning, trainees become physically fit, and perhaps most important, form emotional bonds that help keep up morale when the going is hard.

(*Source*: Partnership for a Drug-Free America)

Participation in self-help support programs during and following treatment often is helpful in maintaining abstinence.

Governments and people are working to help those affected by and those who might become affected by DXM and other OTC drugs. However, the issue of OTC drug abuse is subject to much controversy.

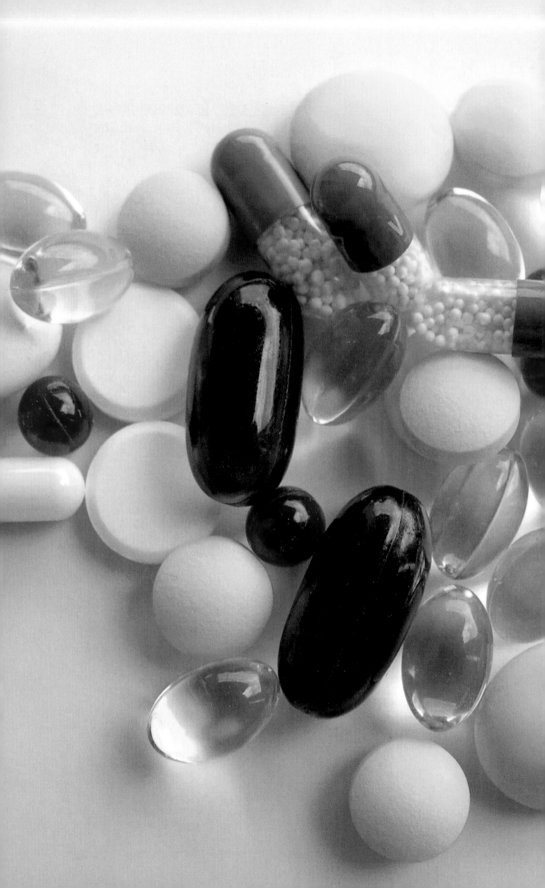

6 Controversial Issues

Legality is the major issue surrounding OTC drugs. Today, these drugs hold a unique position in societies concerned with drug use. Although OTC drugs have been used safely and efficiently by millions of people, the fact that they are being increasingly abused— with deadly consequences—has led some people to question whether their sale should remain unregulated.

The Role of Drug Companies

Some people feel that the drug companies that produce OTC medicines such as cough syrups are the ones who should be fighting against the abuse of their products. So far, some companies have shown that they are willing to work towards limiting OTC drug abuse, but haven't agreed to remove their products from OTC availability. Having the drugs available without the need for a prescription brings the drug companies a lot of income after all. Instead, they work with organizations to fight against

Some drug companies are working with schools to use education as a tool to fight the abuse of OTC medications.

abuse through media campaigns or take their own initiatives to try to stop teens from buying products containing DXM.

One drug company, Wyeth Consumer Healthcare, has designed the packaging of one of its cough products to deter teenagers from abusing it. The medicine comes in a package too large to conveniently hide in a backpack or pocket, thereby serving as a disincentive to abuse that particular product. Some companies gear their actions toward the media and education. Wyeth advertises its products on TV shows for adults, hopefully bypassing the hours and types of programs that most teens are watching. The maker of Coricidin, Schering-Plough, distributed pamphlets to parents and pharmacies, containing information about DXM abuse. Representatives from the company also met with pharmacists, schools, and retailers to discuss abuse.

The Role of the Government

Since the government regulates the sale and use of other drugs, some argue that it should do the same with OTC drugs. It appears that the government is responding to the increased talk of DXM abuse, at least on the state level. The fact that the majority of people who use OTC drugs use them wisely and for legitimate medical reasons makes the situation complicated and one that is not easily addressed by regulation. The needs of people who use OTC drugs safely must be balanced with abuse and its consequences.

People who are alarmed by the harmful ingredients found in dietary supplements advocate stricter governmental regulation of those substances. They are not satisfied that supplements are classified as foods and thereby subject to milder rules than substances classified as drugs. The FDA took an important step in recognizing the danger of ephedra and acting to ban products containing it, but for many people, that is not enough.

Canada currently has a system of harsher regulations of natural health products, that country's classification for dietary supplements. In 2004, the government formally began regulating natural health products under the Natural Health Products Directorate (NHPD). The NHPD maintains certain safety and quality levels that manufacturers of dietary supplements must meet. Many in the United States would like the FDA to adopt a similar practice.

The Internet and DXM Culture

There can be no underestimating the role of the Internet in the abuse of OTC drugs today. The number of Web sites devoted to telling users how to get—and use most effectively—substances like DXM continues to grow. But the issue isn't quite as simple as blaming the Internet for the prevalence of the abuse. DXM abuse was occurring with pockets of devoted followers during the 1970s and 1980s, long before the Internet and its popularity. So while the Internet can be held responsible for informing more people about DXM and its abuse, it did not introduce it to society in general.

There is even discussion about whether or not Internet sites promoting DXM abuse are purely harmful. Most of the sites caution users, providing them with information about the negative consequences of taking DXM and advising them on safe amounts to take, in addition to advice on how to get high. Some argue that teenagers who abuse DXM would be likely to do it whether or not

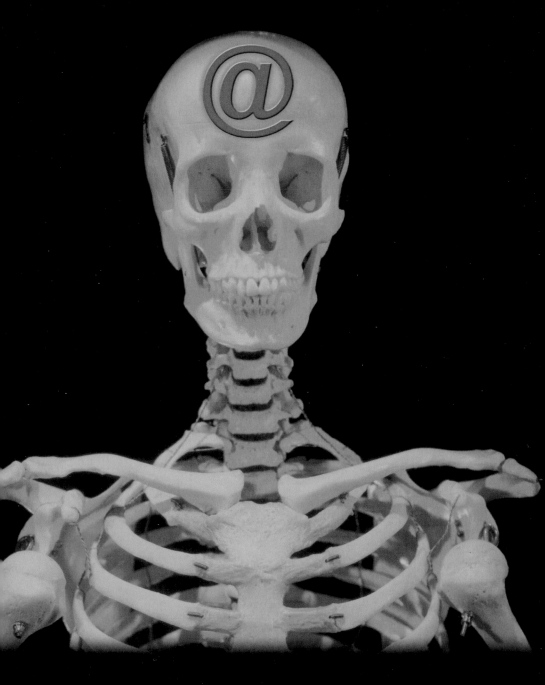

Many people blame the Internet for spreading dangerous knowledge about DXM abuse. Others, however, point out that the Internet can also be a source for knowledge that may promote safer practices among teens.

Abusing Over-the-Counter Drugs 113

Television advertisements designed to fight DXM abuse may instead make young people aware of possibilities for drug use that they had not previously considered.

114 Chapter 6—Controversial Issues

Scientific Definitions

Talking about addiction and dependence can be confusing, because different people use the words to mean different things. According to most scientists: *addiction is a primary, chronic, neurobiological disease, with genetic, psychosocial, and environmental factors influencing its development and manifestations. It is characterized by behaviors that include one or more of the following:*

- *impaired control over drug use*
- *compulsive use*
- *continued use despite harm, and craving.*

The American Psychiatric Association (APA) and the World Health Organization (WHO) use the word "dependence" for the same concept. A more common definition for physical dependence, however, is this:

A state of adaptation that is manifested by a drug class specific withdrawal syndrome that can be produced by abrupt cessation, rapid dose reduction, decreasing blood level of drug and/or administration of an antagonist and is relieved by the readministration of the drug or another drug of the same pharmacologic class.

they had information on the Internet, so if they also had access to information on how to do it relatively safely, should pro-DXM sites be automatically condemned? Of course, other people argue that the sites are advocating drug abuse, no matter how concerned about users' safety they seem to be.

A similar question concerning the media has arisen as well. One of the reasons that DXM abuse has not exploded into the general culture is that the number of people aware of it remains relatively small. Media campaigns against DXM abuse will increase the public's awareness of the problem. They also have the potential of bringing the idea of abusing DXM to the attention of someone who might not otherwise have thought of abusing the drug. The benefits and risks of educating parents and teens about the dangers involved with abusing cough medicines must be weighed; will the benefits outweigh the risks, making such campaigns worthwhile?

Is DXM Really Addictive?

While there is no question of whether or not DXM is being abused, there is speculation as to whether or not that abuse leads to addiction. There is evidence that DXM abuse causes emotional dependence, since users report that they feel the need to take more of it and that some find it hard to quit abuse. There is also some evidence that abuse can cause physical addiction to some degree. One sign of physical addiction to a substance is the appearance of withdrawal symptoms when quitting. Some users experience a mild form of withdrawal after stopping their abuse of DXM, including insomnia and some depression. Limited clinical tests suggest that physical dependence only occurs after DXM is used heavily for a long period of time, not when it is used for short periods of time and with light use. As OTC drug abuse is being brought to light, more research will be done concerning addiction and possibly recovery.

It should also be understood that there is no danger of DXM addiction when using cough syrups and pills as medically indicated. Regular doses of DXM do not cause addiction.

The Fight Against OTC Drug Abuse

People are finally beginning to pay attention to OTC drug abuse in today's world. While there have been few

DXM is not addictive in the same way that nicotine and illegal drugs are. This does not mean, however, that DXM abuse is not a dangerous practice.

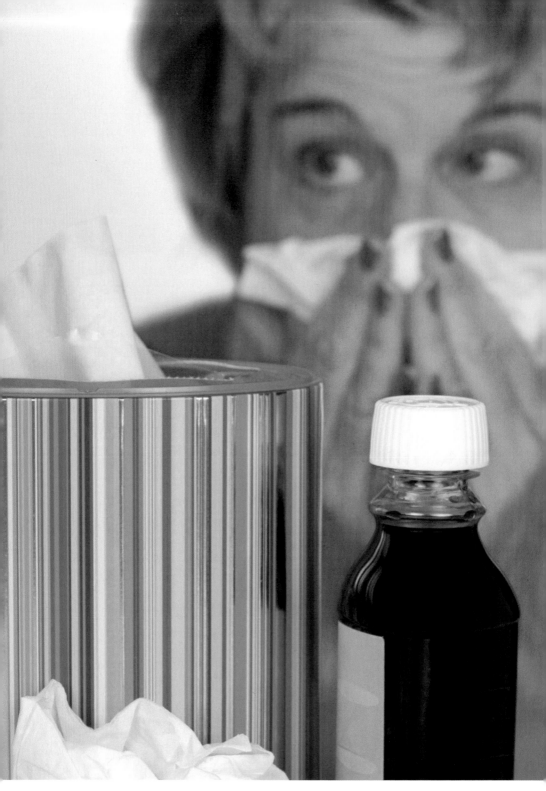

When medications containing DXM are used as they were intended—to treat colds and coughs—there is no risk of them being addictive.

commercials informing people of the problem, few if any brochures found in doctors' offices, and very little informational advertisements in magazines, that is slowly changing. Starting in 2003, the Partnership for a Drug-Free America and the Consumer Healthcare Products Association (CHPA) launched a program to spread knowledge of OTC drug abuse. Their aim was to educate parents about abuse, especially that of cough medicines. In May 2006, the Partnership and CHPA added a communications aspect to their plan. It involves separate Web sites for parents and teens; a television, radio, magazine, and newspaper ad campaign; and a pamphlet printed in both English and Spanish titled, A Parent's Guide to Preventing Teen Cough Medicine Abuse.

The two organizations are also trying to accomplish legal goals. They are focusing on federal laws that would prohibit the sale of pure DXM to anyone not registered with the FDA, much like some state laws already in place. They are also working toward restricting sales of DXM-containing cough medicines to consumers under eighteen.

Organizations like the Partnership for a Drug-Free America and CHPA are paving the way for a new chapter in OTC drug abuse. While OTC drug abuse has long been an underground drug movement, it is now being brought to the public's attention for good or for bad. As more research is done and more knowledge is gained, the problem of OTC drug abuse will be tackled in different ways. For now, their legality and legitimate and safe medical use vies with the dangers inherent in improper use. They inhabit a unique place in the dilemmas of drug abuse, and must be dealt with uniquely.

Glossary

acute: Extremely serious, severe, or painful.

analgesics: Medications that alleviate pain without causing a loss of consciousness.

attributes: Characteristics.

clandestinely: Secretively, usually illegally.

clinical trials: Research done to determine the effectiveness of a medication.

codeine: A white powder derived from opium, but milder in action, used as a painkiller and to relieve coughing.

condoned: Regarded something that is considered immoral or wrong in a tolerant way, without criticizing it or feeling strongly about it.

dehydration: The process of removing moisture from something.

detrimental: Causing harm or damage.

disorientation: Feeling lost or confused.

endorse: To give formal approval or permission for something.

euphoria: Extreme happiness.

extract: A substance obtained from a compound in solid, liquid, or gas form by using an industrial or chemical process.

extremities: Hands and feet.

exude: To communicate a particular quality or feeling in abundance.

genes: The basic units capable of transmitting characteristics from one generation to the next.

hallucinate: To see, hear, or otherwise sense people, things, or events that are not present or actually occurring at the time.

histamines: Compounds released by the immune system during allergic reactions that cause irritation, contraction of smooth muscle, stimulation of gastric secretions, and dilation of the blood vessels.

hypertension: High blood pressure.

idealized: Thought of someone or something as being perfect, ignoring any imperfections.

ketamine: A white powder used as a general anesthetic in human and veterinary medicine.

mania: A psychiatric disorder characterized by excessive physical activity, rapidly changing ideas, and impulsive behavior.

metabolism: The ongoing chemical interactions taking place in living organisms that provide energy and nutrients necessary to sustain life.

metabolize: To undergo metabolism.

paranoia: Extreme and unreasonable suspicion of people and their motives.

patent medicines: Medicines that can be bought without a prescription and are protected by a patent or trademark.

PCP: Phencyclidin; a drug used as an anesthetic in veterinary medicine and illegally as a hallucinogen.

pharmacological: Relating to the science or study of drugs, including their sources, chemistry, production, use in treating diseases, and side effects.

potent: Powerful or strong.

precursor: Something or someone that comes before and leads to the development of another thing or person.

profile: A list of characteristics that indicates the extent to which something matches a standard.

profound: Very great, strong, or intense.

Reye's syndrome: A rare and serious childhood disease, usually following a respiratory infection, causing vomiting, fatty deposits in the liver, disorientation, and swelling of the kidneys and brain.

stimulant: A drug or other agent that produces a temporary increase in functional activity of a body organ or part.

synergistic: Used to describe the working together of two or more things or people, especially when the result is greater than the sum of their individual effects or capabilities.

synthetic: Made artificially.

unattainable: Unreachable.

Further Reading

Bird, Stephen, and B. Joan McClure. *Diet Pills and Other Over-the-Counter Drugs.* New York: Chelsea House, 1999.

Ford, Jean, with Autumn Libal. *The Truth About Diets: The Pros and Cons.* Broomall, Pa.: Mason Crest, 2005.

Ginther, Catherine (ed.). *Drug Abuse SourceBook.* Detroit, Mich.: Omnigraphics, 2004.

Inaba, Darryl, and William Cohen. *Uppers, Downers, All Arounders.* Ashland, Ore.: CNS Publications, 2003.

Klosterman, Lorrie. *Facts About Over-the-Counter Drugs.* New York: Benchmark, 2006.

Lawton, Sandra Augustyn. *Drug Information for Teens.* Detroit, Mich.: Omnigraphics, 2006.

Walker, Pam. *Understanding the Risks of Diet Drugs.* New York: Rosen, 2000.

For More Information

Consumer Healthcare Products Association
www.chpa-info.org/ChpaPortal/PressRoom/FAQs/
   Dextromethorphan.htm

Focus Adolescent Services
www.focusas.com/SubstanceAbuse.html

Go Ask Alice
www.goaskalice.columbia.edu

Health Canada
www.hc-sc.gc.ca/index_e.html

Parents. The Anti-Drug.
www.theantidrug.com

The Partnership for a Drug-Free America
www.drugfree.org/Parent
Parents: www.drugfree.org/dxm
Teens: www.dxmstories.com

Rader Programs—Specializing in the Treatment of Anorexia,
Bulimia, and Compulsive Overeating
www.raderprograms.com/index.aspx

Teen Drug Abuse
www.teendrugabuse.us/over_the_counter_drug_abuse.html

Bibliography

CESAR—Center for Substance Abuse Research. http://www.cesar.umd.edu/cesar/drugs/dxm.asp.

Coalitions Online. http://cadca.org/CoalitionsOnline/default.asp.

ContinuingEducation.com. http://www.continuingeducation.com/pharmacy/dextro/abuse.html.

Drugs and Human Performance Fact Sheets. http://www.nhtsa.dot.gov/people/injury/research/job185drugs/dextromethorphan.htm.

Erowid. http://www.erowid.org/chemicals/dxm/dxm.shtml..

Greater Dallas Council on Alcohol & Drug Abuse. http://www.gdcada.org/statistics/dxm.htm.

Medical News Today. http://www.medicalnewstoday.com/medicalnews.php?newsid=5072.

MedicineNet.com.http://www.medicinenet.com/script/main/hp.asp.

Mirror-Mirror—Eating Disorders. http://www.mirror-mirror.org/dangerou.htm.

National Center for Complementary and Alternative Medicine. http://nccam.nih.gov/health/alerts/ephedra/consumeradvisory.htm.

The National Drug Intelligence Center. http://www.usdoj.gov/ndic/pubs11/11563/index.htm.

Office of Dietary Supplements. http://ods.od.nih.gov/factsheets/DietarySupplements.asp.

www.streetdrugs.org. http://www.streetdrugs.org/otc.htm.

The Tox. http://www.toxi.ch/eng/news_957184695_28669.html.

Index

Picture Credits

BKDesign: p. 23
CJRFoto: p. 30
FDA: p. 47
Fotolia
    Allen, Joseph: p.11
    Blazic, Ana: p. 67
    Brzostowska, Maria: p. 105
    Cosmin, Mosca: p. 72
    Date, Philip: p. 54
    Docken, Cory: p. 8
    Godfer: p. 58
    Haulbaekdal, Anne: p. 13
    Hermans, Stefan: p. 24
    Hurst, Ken: p. 26
    Kostic, Zlatco: p. 63
    Leach, V.: p. 101
    Kulkarni, Makarand: p. 110
    Marozova, Tatiana: p .51
    Ottaviano, Silvia: p. 83
    Tandel, Stephan: p. 78
    Thompson, Michael: p. 77
    Vanweddingen, Vincent: p. 80
    Wariatka, Matka: p. 14
iStockphotos
    Clapper, Cathleen: p. 117
    Gordon, Kurt: p. 108
    Masse, Isabel: p. 98
    Mockel, Felix: p. 102
    Pargeter Kristy: p. 68
    Pridhodko, Olga: pp. 60, 88
    Stay, Mark: p. 86
Jedphoto: p. 113
Jupiter Images: pp. 16, 19, 20, 36, 48, 56, 74, 91, 92, 94, 97
Kaulitzki, Sebastian: pp. 28, 84
Stockphotonyc: p. 114
U.S. National Library of Medicine: pp. 38, 41, 42, 45

To the best knowledge of the publisher, all other images are in the public domain. If any image has been inadvertently uncredited, please notify Harding House Publishing Service, Vestal, New York 13850, so that rectification can be made for future printings.

Author and Consultant Biographies

Author

Kim Etingoff has contributed to a small local newspaper, where she worked as editor in chief for the past year. She is currently furthering her education at the University of Rochester in New York State. Kim is also the author of several other nonfiction young adult books published by Mason Crest.

Series Consultant

Jack E. Henningfield, Ph.D., is a professor at the Johns Hopkins University School of Medicine, and he is also Vice President for Research and Health Policy at Pinney Associates, a consulting firm in Bethesda, Maryland, that specializes in science policy and regulatory issues concerning public health, medications development, and behavior-focused disease management. Dr. Henningfield has contributed information relating to addiction to numerous reports of the U.S. Surgeon General, the National Academy of Sciences, and the World Health Organization.